Haunted Bedfordshire - A Gl

Haunted Bedfordshire

A Ghostly Compendium

William H. King

First published November 2005

The Book Castle
12 Church Street
Dunstable
Bedfordshire LU5 4RU

ISBN 1-903747-63-5
ISBN 9781903747636

Cover Design by William H. King

To my son and daughter who joined me on many an investigation.

I really appreciated your being there.

Contents

Contents

Introduction

This book is a compilation of many of the ghost stories and legends that abound in Bedfordshire. The list is extensive with over one hundred and forty separate haunted sites and paranormal events being recorded herein. But this is not all of them; each day I find more tales so that the list grows, but this book is at least a start.

Each site is listed alphabetically along with details of what has occurred there, as well as visit reports for a few of the sites. I have not included all of the visit reports as they would occupy a book unto themselves and most are not particularly eventful. In addition to the site details I have included the British National Grid coordinates of the site to enable you to locate it. Using these and an Ordnance Survey map of the area you can easily locate the site. The grid reference is accurate for most sites where the exact location is known, but for others it just gets you into the right area.

I cannot claim that everything in this book is accurate. I try to be as accurate as possible and will give different versions of a haunting if the data is available. Like all good stories they may have changed with the passage of time; some will have been embellished and for others the fine detail will have been lost. I have also visited all of the sites at some time, so I know where they are and what they are like.

Have I seen a ghost? My earliest recollection is when I was a teenager about fifteen years of age. I used to live in a small village in Worcestershire and had a two mile walk to school. Part of that walk was across a field used as a recreation ground and football pitch. I used to walk home across this field from one corner by a road to the opposite corner where there was a path. The road was reasonably well lit, but the opposite corner was utterly black as there were only a few houses nearby then open countryside. I remember that it was the middle of winter and I was walking home in the dark. It was a dry evening with no snow on the ground and the air was clear. I had walked about a quarter of the way across the field when I saw what appeared to be a large white dog about fifty metres in front of me. It had the appearance of a German Shepherd Dog and appeared to be alone as I could see no sign of the owner, though they could easily have been across the field in the darkness. At the time I thought the dog looked unusually light as there were no street lights nearby. The next second it was suddenly just not there. One second I could see it and the next second it was gone, but there was nowhere for it to go. At the time I was a rational teenager studying for my 'O' levels who was very into science (so much so that I went on to get an Honours degree at university studying Astrophysics). Yet I saw something I could not explain. The 'dog' had vanished but it had nowhere to go.

Today, thirty years on, I do not see ghosts for the sake of seeing them; I do not take photographs and say that every spot of light is an orb (see Chapter 4). I try to explain everything away rationally, but there are some things I cannot explain. 'I suspect that there are more things in Heaven and Earth than are dreamed of, or can be dreamed of, in any philosophy.' It is these things that I seek. I believe in ghosts, be they recordings of past events or the spirits of the departed. I want to know what they are and this is what interests me. The quest for an explanation is a long one but a fascinating one and it is one that I will follow for as long as I can. The paranormal fascinates me and long may it do so.

I have also heard things that I cannot explain, even though I try to explain them away. During a recent all night vigil with members of the Luton Paranormal Society I did two sound recordings, both of which contained brief sounds which I am unable to explain. The first was a demonic laugh superimposed on the sound of two people talking and the second was a distant voice crying "Get out! Get out!" This is what drives me. I am fascinated by the unknown and certainly not frightened of it (I am more inclined to go up and poke a ghost to see what it is made of than flee from it in terror, what is there to be afraid of?).

Ghosts have been seen for thousands of years and one day I believe we will be able to explain what we see, once we can really open our minds and avoid the narrow minded views of modern society.

Bedfordshire

Chapter 1

Towns and Villages

Throughout this book coordinates are given for each site to enable you to locate it. The coordinates are the British National Grid reference, which allows you to locate any place in the United Kingdom, with an accuracy dependent on the number of digits in the coordinate. A typical reference would look like TL103484 or TL10374844. The first coordinate gets you to a place with an accuracy of one hundred metres; the second coordinate is accurate to ten metres. Some coordinates are given with six digits if the exact location is unknown (usually when the haunting is along a road). Other coordinates are given with eight digits when the location is known (usually a building). The coordinates may not represent the middle of a building, but they will correspond to the nearest access point (end of a private drive etc.). For further details and an explanation of how the system works see the appendix.

AMPTHILL

The name Ampthill is derived from the Anglo-Saxon *Aemethyll* which, unfortunately, means an ant-infested hill.

The town had very close associations with King Henry VIII as he often brought his court to Ampthill Castle. The castle no longer exists and the land it stood on is now Ampthill Great Park, with the site of the castle being marked by the Katherine Cross. Henry VIII's first wife, Katherine of Aragon, stayed at the castle while her twenty year marriage to Henry was annulled. It is after her that the cross is named.

In Kit William's book 'Masquerade' the location of a golden, jewel encrusted hare was given for any with the ability to find it from the clues given. The hare was supposedly buried at the base of the Katherine Cross.

The town contains several Tudor buildings and numerous others from the seventeenth and eighteenth centuries. The parish church has a monument to Richard Nicholls who took New Amsterdam from the Dutch in 1664 and renamed it New York.

Chandos Road

In August 1987 a report appeared in the 'Ampthill and Flitwick Times' about a haunting in Chandos Road, Ampthill, where strange events had been going on for nineteen years from the time that a family first moved to the house. The owners described a mischievous ghost who used to hide items; these included spectacles, cutlery, jam and jumpers. In the house a sliding door was seen to move by itself even though it was very heavy, and items including bowls and bread would fall off shelves of their own accord. Eventually the children gave the spirit a name, Mrs. Farr. They later discovered that a Miss Elizah Parr had once been housekeeper there and that she had died in August 1932. Elizah, also known as Totty, worked in the White Hart at Ampthill as a chambermaid

2

at the turn of the nineteenth century before moving to Chandos Road. It appears that Elizah had been involved in a scandal whilst she was at the White Hart, a scandal involving an illegitimate child.

One chair in the Chandos Road house was reserved for Elizah but most of the incidences took place in the kitchen where Elizah must have spent a large part of her time when she was alive. One of her favourite 'thefts' was strawberry jam; this would later return to the table by itself.

Elizah was a very quiet ghost who made no noise, though she was seen twice. The first sighting was by the youngest daughter of the family, who was surprised to see an unknown woman standing in the window. The second time Elizah was seen was by the father, who said that he saw something at the end of the upstairs corridor which appeared to be a figure wearing a long skirt.

Grid reference: TL033379

Church Street

The 'Bedfordshire on Sunday' newspaper once carried a story of a haunted hairdresser's, '1710 Hair Design and Beauty', in Church Street, Ampthill. It was reported to have been haunted by at least two ghosts. One customer was said to have seen the image of a hanged man in an upstairs room.

The owner eventually decided that enough was enough and called in exorcists. This resulted in an end to that particular haunting. Even though the hanged man was gone, a small boy was still seen regularly by staff and customers, again upstairs. The owner said that she felt as if there was something upstairs but she couldn't say what it was. All she did know was that it was not a place to be on your own.

Grid reference: TL035381

Great Park

Ampthill Great Park was landscaped by 'Capability' Brown and occupies a one hundred and twenty hectare site to the north-west of the town of Ampthill. In the park a ghost has been seen that must rank as one of the most memorable in Bedfordshire. The ghost was described as a "knight in full armour with a plumed helmet, riding a glorious white steed". A full account was given in 1965 by an ex-policeman who was holidaying in the area. Whilst walking through the park with his family he

saw "the vague shape of a man on a horse who suddenly appeared from where the castle used to be and then vanished near a small brook".

No records exist to explain who this rider may have been or why he now haunts this area, though his emergence does correspond with the original location of the castle, which is now marked by Katherine's Cross (grid reference: TL02473840). Erected in 1737 this memorial cross was dedicated to Katherine of Aragon, who lived for a while in the castle while her marriage to Henry VIII was being annulled (see the picture above).

The Castle was built by John Cornwall (later to become Lord Fanhope) in the fifteenth century after his marriage to Princess Elizabeth. The building work was financed from the spoils of the war with France. Following his death, John's friend Ralph, Lord Cromwell, made a claim for the castle, but it was seized from him by Cornwall's stepson, the Duke of Exeter. Later it came into the possession of Lord Grey of Ruthin, who kept it until mounting debts forced him to give it to the King, Henry VIII. From around 1524 it became one of Henry VIII's royal palaces and he would use it to escape the unhealthy atmosphere in London during the summer months of July and August. Whilst staying in the castle he would follow one of the great pleasures of his life, hunting, for which the great park was very suitable. In 1528 he stayed at the castle with Anne Boleyn and other members of his court.

After Henry died the castle quickly fell into decay, with local people using some of the materials in their own buildings. Large parts of the original castle were put into storage and then later used in other royal buildings. In the late seventeenth century the Great Lodge was rebuilt on a very grand scale by Lord Ashburnham. Following a brief spell as a Cheshire Home after WWII it was converted into three separate dwellings. Finally, in 1948, the Urban District Council of Ampthill purchased the Great Park and its woods and it remains today as a public park managed by Ampthill Town Council.

There are two crosses in the park; the first, Katherine's Cross, has already been mentioned, whilst the second cross, pictured above, is the

Ampthill Camp Memorial Cross (grid reference: TL02573835). This cross was erected to commemorate the soldiers who were trained in a camp which had been set up in the park and who, like so many others, never returned from the First World War.

The entrance to the park can be found one kilometre outside Ampthill. Follow the B530 west from the town centre; the entrance lies on the right just before the junction with the A507 (grid reference: TL02413813). A short driveway leads to the car park.

Grid reference: TL025384

Houghton House

In 1915 a resident of Ampthill was returning home from doing war work in a Luton factory to the small farm where her parents lived. Suddenly she heard the sound of horses' hooves coming along the narrow lane on which she was walking. Fearing she would be injured she threw

herself into a ditch. As she lay there she heard the pounding of the horses' hooves and the jingling of harnesses as if a great coach was passing her by on the way to Houghton House, but when she looked there was nothing there.

Houghton House lies to the north-east of Ampthill and was built in 1615 for the Countess of Pembroke, later becoming the home of the Bruce family. Unfortunately for the Bruces they took the wrong side during the civil war and ended up locked in the Tower of London. The house was then bought by the Duke of Bedford in 1738, and by 1794 he was having it dismantled. In the Swan Hotel in Bedford can still be seen the great staircase which came from Houghton House. In the 1930s local people raised money to save the building and it is now in the care of English Heritage.

The site is accessed from a sign-posted concrete road off the B530 approximately seven hundred metres north of the centre of Ampthill (grid reference: TL03273879). The B530 climbs a steep hill then turns sharply to the right; as you come out of this right-hand bend you will see a signpost on the left and the driveway to the house on the right. About nine hundred metres along this road there is a car park on the left just before a row of cottages. The house lies along a tree lined path which starts three hundred metres to the north past the cottages and left at the farm buildings.

Houghton House is believed to have been the inspiration for 'House Beautiful' in John Bunyan's 'The Pilgrim's Progress'. Certainly a painting of the house, done at the time of its heyday, shows it to have been a very elegant and ornate property.

Grid reference: TL03923946

Site Report

Houghton House is an excellent site to visit, especially if you like ruined houses. Apart from being a marvellous old ruin it is very quiet, save for the occasional noises from the local farm, and it is dark, as the nearest lights come from just a few cottages across the fields. The house lies on an isolated hill high above Marston Vale and is a wonderful location both by night and by day. During the day there are excellent views across the vale.

The only reported haunting took place along a path to the ruin and involved the sound of a coach and horses. Any coach would have been approaching the house along the original driveway but this no longer exists. As you drive along the concrete road to the car park, if you look right you will see a walled garden (if it's not too dark). If this is the original garden (now Lodge Piece Farm), then it used to lie alongside the road to the house. The line of the road (now the John Bunyan Trail) skirted the east end of the cottages which lie alongside the road you take from the car park to the site entrance. The entrance

to the site lies directly in line with the John Bunyan Trail as a tree lined avenue. As the trail and the avenue run along the top of a ridge, straight to the main entrance of the house, it seems very likely that this was the route that the phantom coach had been taking.

I have visited the site several times at night, usually about one o'clock in the morning. The first time was a dry night but the second

8

time, in March 2004, there was blustery rain, which led to some interesting photographs. The site is very open atop a hill so it is usually windy, which can make it unpleasant on a wet day. A lot of the building still remains but it is open to the elements (the roof went a long time ago). There is some vandalism (graffiti), though there is fortunately very little, and it does not detract from the general look of the site.

I spent some time wandering around both outside and inside the ruin but saw nothing interesting. Of the numerous photographs taken that night, the image on the previous page is a typical example. When you look at the image there appear to be several orbs and some strange bright streaks. To a lot of people these are spirit orbs and proof of the continuation of the soul. Alas, the cause of all of these is the rain and mist that was around that night, as will be discussed in the chapter on 'Orbs' (Chapter 4).

Main Street

In the second half of the nineteenth century a couple moved into a house which lay just off Ampthill's main thoroughfare. It wasn't long before they began to experience paranormal phenomena of a most disturbing nature. It all started when they were both in bed and the bedroom door suddenly opened wide and 'something' entered. They could hear the sounds of someone staggering around the room and gasping, then the words "Pull it out, please pull it out". This was followed by more gasps, the sounds of someone in a great deal of pain and finally a most terrible, soul wrenching scream.

It transpired that the couple were friendly with Bill Turner, Bedfordshire's first real paranormal investigator. Around 1870 Bill stayed at the house to help them tidy up the garden and while he was there he was told the story of the ghost. The above event repeated itself to Bill's friends before Bill finally heard it for himself. Bill related the events to the owner of the property, Mrs. Letitia Bland, and she eventually told him the grisly tale behind the haunting.

About twenty years previously Mrs. Anne Rumbelow and her daughter Agnes, who was aged fifteen at the time, had lived in the house. One night they heard sounds coming from the garden and Agnes had run downstairs to make sure the house was secure. Minutes later she staggered into her mother's room screaming "Pull it out!" To her mother's horror she found a sickle embedded in Agnes' back. Agnes survived the night but died the next day. Her murderer was never found. Since then the house has been haunted by Agnes re-enacting her agony as she staggered into her mother's bedroom with the sickle in her back.

Grid reference: TL034381

The White Hart

In the White Hart hotel in Dunstable Street there is a room which is supposedly haunted; conveniently the room is number thirteen. The White Hart is an old hotel with parts of the building dating back to the fifteenth century; not least the route to Room 13 which climbs two flights of wooden stairs, followed by a corridor under the roof where the old beams can be seen. In the year 2000 a team of reporters from 'The Bedfordshire Times' spent the night in Room 13 investigating the phenomena. One of the first things they noticed was that the door at the end of the corridor was propped open with an ironing board; they were told that this was for the ghost. The room itself was bare as it was rarely used. That night nothing happened within the room but this was not the case in the bar. At ten o'clock while they were sitting in the back bar, the window suddenly flew open against the prevailing wind. One reporter, who was standing next to the window at the time, maintained that no human could have opened it, especially as it lay twenty feet above the courtyard below.

A regular at the hotel said that he'd had two previous encounters with ghosts there. Once he tried to close the door that is usually propped open, against the advice of his wife who was a cleaner at the hotel. As he closed the door it suddenly swung open and hit him on the head. According to his wife 'she' doesn't like it closed. The second occurrence happened when the witness was in the bar. In this instance he observed a

gentleman wearing a top hat walk in through the main door, cross the bar then suddenly vanish. The regular, Frank, wasn't the only witness to this event as at least two or three other people in the bar saw it too. The ghost was reported as looking like an old coachman wearing a cape.

The landlord at the time, Shea Keegan, was convinced that the ghost exists and even reckoned there was definitely more than one ghost there. He was aided in his belief when he saw glasses moving around the bar of their own accord in the middle of the night. Members of the Luton Paranormal Society were lucky to be able to investigate the White Hart and they obtained some interesting results.

Grid reference: TL03483811

Site Report

In July 2004 the White Hart hotel in Ampthill was investigated by members of the Luton Paranormal Society (LPS). On July 6th 2001 a fire had badly damaged the top floor of the building and repair/modernisation was almost complete. It was felt that this was a good time to investigate the building as existing paranormal activity can increase, and new activity can start, when a building is being modified.

The investigation started at eleven o'clock in the evening with LPS splitting up into three teams of four. Each team spent approximately one hour in a particular room before moving on. During the time spent there the teams were also joined by some members of the White Hart staff. The following is a report of that investigation by one of the teams.

Room 1 – Edith Bray's Chamber

Like all rooms in the hotel this one was bare of furnishings but complete with en suite shower. A general plan of the rooms in the area is shown in the diagram on the right (this is not to scale). At first only the four LPS members were present but they were later joined by two members of the pub staff. The two staff members remained in the room for about twenty minutes, then left. The male staff member said that LPS should visit the room at the end of the corridor (labelled Room 2 on the diagram).

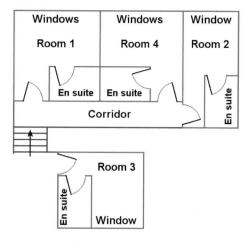

on the diagram). He also said about the ghost of a child which is believed to be Katherine of Aragon's daughter (later to become Queen Mary I, though some say it is Anne Boleyn's daughter, later to become Queen Elizabeth I).

LPS occupied the room from 1130 until 0025, which is not a recommended time slot as the room was very noisy due to people using the inn below. Initial temperature readings were +22°C in the room and +20.5°C near the window. The room is very bright due to streetlights in Dunstable Street and Woburn Street. No one felt anything strange about the room during the time LPS were in there. Nothing was heard, but a tape recording which was made over a period of forty-five minutes did contain one set of sounds the origin of which is unknown. In the recording you can hear one of the LPS members talking to the male member of the White Hart staff, then the strange sound can be heard, almost like a demonic laugh. At the time the recorder was placed in the bottom left corner of Room 1 on a ledge; no one was near it as all of the occupants of the room were down by the windows. I was present during this recording and distinctly remember the conversation and where people were at the time. I also remember that there were no strange sounds at the time, including natural ones like coughing etc.

Nothing showed up on photographs except a few dust orbs. One general note: the inn has room doors which close slowly of their own accord until there are just a couple of centimetres to go, then they slam shut. This generates a lot of noise which can be heard throughout the Inn. In addition all of the floors creak, partially due to the old nature of the building and partially due to the extra boarding attached to the floorboards to try to level them.

Room 2 – Gatehouse Chamber

Apart from a brief period at the start of the 0040 to 0140 vigil there was too much of a disturbance going on in the street outside to have made any time in this room meaningful. Initial temperature was measured at +21.5°C over the whole room. A trigger object, in this case a cross with its outline drawn on paper, was left in the shower. To ensure no living person meddled with it the shower cubicle door was subtly marked, so that it could be seen if it had been opened. When the cross was collected at 5 am, it was found that it had not moved, though the two marks on the door were very slightly misaligned. The movement of the door could easily have been caused by vibrations as people moved around.

This room is again a very light one due to the street lights outside. When LPS first entered the room the window was closed and there was a distinct smell to the room which one LPS member reckoned was cigarette smoke. After a while, and with the aid of an open window, this dispersed.

Again the only things on photographs were a few dust orbs and no strange feelings were felt whilst the room was occupied.

Room 3 – The Red Chamber

This room is unusual as it has an oak beamed wall; LPS occupied it from about 0145 to 0300. Again this room felt OK and showed a fairly constant +21.5°C the entire time LPS were in there. One thing which made the investigation difficult at the start was the constant light flashes which were seen on the ceiling due to photographs being taken downstairs in the bar area.

During the time LPS were in the room they tried ten minutes of silence so that they could record any sounds in the room but a later review of the tape revealed nothing. At one point one LPS member said that she had seen a shadow silently pass the door. Her partner confirmed that he had seen the same out of the corner of his eye. To try to find out what could have caused this one team member went outside the room and walked back and forth. At no point could he reproduce the effect that had been seen without walking right up against the door though this meant that, unnaturally, he had to walk into the wall which lies to the left of the door.

Bright spots of light had been reported by a previous group, and while LPS were in there one of the team saw a total of nine light effects which all occurred in the first half of the hour. One LPS member sat on the window ledge whilst two other members sat beneath the wooden wall (directly opposite the window). The observer of the anomalies sat to the right of the window (as you face it) and all of the occurrences were observed in the direction of the wooden wall.

The light effects included:

- •A bright patch of red light to the right of the female LPS member's head, almost like a halo.
- •A red blob in the far right corner of the wooden wall and about 2 metres off the ground.
- •A purple blob, in similar position to the red blob, but to the right.
- •A streak of white about 15 cm long which appeared to be one metre off the ground and half way to the entrance corridor.
- •Six white dots randomly distributed over the far wall.

Photographs were taken facing towards the corner where most of the light anomalies were seen. All that was visible on the images were a few dust orbs and two bright specks which may also have been dust.

Room 4

Whilst in Room 3 LPS decided to place sound recorders in two rooms, one of which they had previously occupied. One was placed in Room 1 and another in Room 4 (placed at about 0230). On the Room 4 recording, which lasted about one and a half hours, there is a strange sound which occurs not long after the other team members had changed rooms. The sound could have come from elsewhere but that does seem unlikely as it is quiet but not distorted as you would expect if the sound came from another room. Some time after 3 am you can hear people moving around and the usual muffled voices that you get when you hear a sound through a wall or floor. Then you can hear, very distinctly, a woman's voice. The voice is not muffled; it is quiet as if it has come from some way away but not through the walls. The voice shouts the words "Get out!" twice.

Cellar

When LPS entered the cellar they had to wait fifteen minutes due to noises coming from above (the bar area) as the other teams dispersed. The general temperature in the cellar was +21°C but one side cellar measured only +17.5 to +19°C. A trigger object (again a cross outlined on paper) was left in the refrigerated room at the end of the cellar. By the end of the night this was found to have moved by about 1.5 mm. The person who had set up the object cannot be certain that he didn't move it but it seems unlikely. The object appears to have been rotated on the paper, with the pencil outline corresponding well with the cross but misaligned. If he had knocked the cross whilst tracing its outline you would have expected part of the outline to be correct and part out of place but this was not the case. The only way for it to have been done would have been for him to have knocked it when he was finishing installing it, but he would have noticed. It is suggested that from now on the trigger object is checked by someone else immediately after it has been set up so that you have an independent witness (including a photograph).

For twenty minutes the LPS member who had seen the lights in Room 3 shut himself away in the side cellar with the door closed. This was done so that the room was pitch-black and he could try to reproduce the bright light effects he had seen in Room 3. As Room 3 had not been totally dark, due to light coming in from outside, he tried various light levels from fully dark to partially lit but he was unable to see the same light flashes. I know he saw the light effects in Room 3 and I know he couldn't reproduce them later in the cellar as in actuality 'he' was 'me'.

Bar Area

The last investigation undertaken by the team was in the bar area, though this was more of a brief check of the trigger objects that had been left there by one of the other teams. One of the objects had shown signs of being moved as shown in the image on the next page. It can be seen that the object has moved about one centimetre, revealing a clear area with no white powder. This object was sitting away from the main bar in a small room to the right of the stairs which lie directly in front of the main entrance to the hotel.

Unfortunately LPS could not guarantee that the object had not been deliberately moved, as the area was not being continuously monitored and people other than LPS members were present in the building. One team did say that the object moved while they were in the bar, though they did not see it move and they were not watching the object all the time. Another object was positioned about seven hundred and fifty millimetres away from the object that had moved, but this one showed no signs of having been disturbed.

One thing about trigger objects is that you must be able to guarantee that they cannot be moved by anyone; otherwise the experiment has no validity. This is especially true when people other than your group members are present. If a trigger object cannot be watched all the time then it is worthwhile setting up a video camera to record the object. The monitoring helps prevent human intervention and, if an object does move, then it would be interesting to have a recording of the event.

ARLESEY

Arlesey is a village with a population of 4,860 lying on the east coast main railway line from London King's Cross to Edinburgh. It is a long thin village where, in the nineteenth century, Gault clay bricks used to be manufactured for use in railway construction.

At the time of the Domesday Book the village was called *Alricesei*. It has been a Royal Manor (*Arleseybury*), a market town and, at one time, the most prosperous parish in the area. Now it is a narrow village extending about five kilometres along the River Hiz.

Lamb Meadow

In 1984 the owner of a house in Lamb Meadow kept having a very disturbing and very vivid dream. The dream always involved a nine year old girl who looked Italian and she would always ask "can I have my daddy back?"

The owner of the house asked her family to say prayers and the dreams stopped, but she still felt as if there was a presence in the house but this time she felt that it was a man. A friend sensed his presence and felt that there was always someone sitting by the stairs. He has also been felt brushing past people.

Grid reference: TL190354

BARTON-LE-CLAY

Barton-le-Clay has a population of 4,090 and lies at the foot of the chalk escarpment that makes up much of the landscape of South Bedfordshire and Luton. The village has given its name to the Barton Hills which offer excellent walks and views.

Barton-le-Clay is a mainly residential area which has seen a large amount of expansion in recent years especially due to its close proximity to Luton. The quiet nature of the village is largely due to the A6 bypass to the west which now diverts much of the traffic away from the village.

Waterside Mill

The Waterside Mill at Barton-le-Clay appears to be haunted by two ghosts. The first was seen by John Duggan when he was leaving the premises which are now a restaurant. He locked up and was just about to drive away when he saw a figure in the window of the mill which seemed to be beckoning for him to return. Thinking he had locked someone in, he went back to the mill and searched all over but could find no one. A week later, again as he was leaving, his car headlights lit up the figure of a woman at a window. He described her as an old woman probably in her eighties. He was especially aware of her long grey hair and her bony hands which were beckoning for him to return.

The second ghost was heard by a visitor to the restaurant. She heard the prolonged crying of a child whilst she was visiting the toilet, but she could not tell where the sound was coming from. At that time there were no children in the restaurant.

Things have also been known to disappear seconds after you have put them down, only to reappear later in a different place. Upstairs in the mill there is a function room at the very top of the building and this is reported to have a very uncomfortable feeling about it. John has also heard footsteps upstairs when the place was empty and his whiskey keeps disappearing, but only nips, not the whole bottle.

The mill site itself has been used since the time of the Domesday Book and, unusually, passed into private ownership in the sixteenth and seventeenth centuries. Eventually the mill passed to Fred Hipgrave after his father, William, and his brother, George, died. Fred sold the rights of the mill and became a tenant but he found it financially crippling. This was made worse by the water levels dropping as more and more wells were dug in Luton.

Fred suffered from chronic depression and, when strong winds blew the cart shed down, the mill wheel broke and the steam engine failed, it became increasing difficult to pay the rent. Fred seems to have had no skills when it came to repairs, so that he was always asking for help until it all became too much. On Wednesday 3rd October 1912 the body of Fred Hipgrave was found by his friend, Simeon Mead, hanging from a beam in the mill house; he was fifty-four years of age. But Fred was a man, so who is the old female ghost?

The mill is very easy to miss as it lies behind trees just off the dual carriageway section of the A6. The entrance to the Waterside Mill

Restaurant and Garden Centre lies three kilometres north of the A6 Streatley roundabout on the left (grid reference: TL07793144) and five hundred metres before the next roundabout. The road to the left is signposted for the local industrial area. Immediately on turning off the A6, turn left along the road which runs back alongside the A6; the mill lies two hundred metres away along this road.

Grid reference: TL07663121

BATTLESDEN

Battlesden is a small village which is easily missed as it does not lie on any road which goes anywhere else. It lies off the Woburn to Hockliffe road in a lane which loops back to the Woburn road. The population in the 1991 census was only thirty-four.

It appears in the Domesday Book as *Badelesdone* or *Badelestone*. Only Battlesden Park now remains of a large manor house which was demolished in 1885. At one time, the park occupied over a hundred hectares of the local countryside, now it has been reduced to just twelve hectares.

Country Lane

In the autumn of 1982 two people were out cycling along a country lane near Battlesden when a disembodied pair of hands suddenly appeared over a hedgerow and proceeded to throw a small log into the road. The log landed directly in front of one of the cyclists, causing them to swerve violently so as to avoid hitting it.

When they looked back there was no sign of the hands and, no matter how much they searched, they could not find anyone in the vicinity who could have thrown the log at them, and no explanation as to why the log was thrown.

To access the village follow the A4012 towards Woburn from Hockliffe. Do not take the first signposted road to Battlesden (just over one and a quarter kilometres from Hockliffe), instead take the second road on your left (grid reference: SP97082966). Follow this narrow road for about one kilometre to reach the village centre.

Grid reference: SP966286

BEDFORD

Bedford originated during the sixth and seventh centuries when it developed as a crossing point over the river Great Ouse. It is thought that the name derives from that of a Saxon Chief, *Beda*, who settled there with his followers. Alfred the Great's son and successor, King Edward the Elder, came to Bedford and ordered the construction of the King's Ditch as a defence against the Danes. The ditch lay to the south of the river and the eastern half remains visible to this day.

The original castle was built shortly after the Norman Conquest of 1066. It was later destroyed in 1224 after a siege which lasted six weeks.

All that now remains is the castle mound which has recently been upgraded to make it more accessible to the public.

John Bunyan began to write his famous book 'The Pilgrim's Progress' whilst he was imprisoned in Bedford Gaol during 1676. A building in the town, known as St. John's House, has incorporated into it the remains of the St. John's hospital which is said to have been the basis for the 'Interpreters House' in 'The Pilgrim's Progress'.

Bedford is now a large town with a population of 74,310. It has plenty of shops and entertainment facilities, including walks along the banks of the river Great Ouse which runs right through the town.

Abbey Middle School

It is said that if you enter the girls' toilets in Abbey Middle School the doors will close by themselves and you will be able to hear the sounds of music and voices. What makes these sounds interesting is that they are not made by anything earthly.

Grid reference: TL05374748

Allhallows

In 1979 near to the Midland Bank (HSBC) in Allhallows, Bedford, shoppers were rather surprised to see a mediaeval friar in his hooded gown. He was calmly walking down the street meditating on his rosary. It seems likely, from the direction in which he was walking, that he had come from Greyfriars which used to be the site of a priory.

This story is so similar to the one headed 'The Greyfriars' that it seems likely that the ghosts are one and the same.

Grid reference: TL04764986

Aspects Leisure Centre

In the Aspects Leisure Complex (UGC Cinema) in Newnham Avenue in Bedford there appears to be both a haunted cinema and, inconveniently, a haunted toilet. Strange happenings have been observed numerous times in Screen 4, including doors violently opening of their own accord, even though the catch was on. Customers have complained of hearing scratching noises coming from above their heads and the feeling of 'phantom' hands on their legs. Seat 8 in row 'A' refuses to stay upright. No matter how many times it is put up, the next instant it is down again, but not straight away, only when no one is watching. Jingling chains have also been heard and that particular theatre is always a lot cooler than any other, never rising above five degrees centigrade even in the summer.

Some years ago an usherette confirmed that her nephew had hung himself from a tree in the grounds of the old priory where Screen 4 now stands. One regular visitor to the cinema, an elderly lady, remembered that the Newnham Swimming Pool used to stand on the site now occupied by the cinema. She also recalled that the lockers would open by themselves then shut with a bang. This would always happen at the same time of night. Things would usually start to happen after half past eleven at night and would normally end at half past seven in the morning when the cleaners arrived.

Other occurrences include a security guard who saw a figure in the foyer even though the cinema was locked up for the night. He was surprised when the figure crossed the foyer and walked straight through the locked doors into the car park. On numerous occasions a figure of a man has been seen in the ladies toilet. The figure is usually seen in the mirror and was once reported to have been wearing monks' clothing. One customer was so frightened she locked herself in a cubicle and later reported that she had seen a man's feet under the door. One other witness was a young girl who was heard screaming in the toilet because of "the man in the mirror". The toilet stands next to Screen 4.

One other employee witnessed several strange things, including a kettle which switched itself back on and boiled, even though it was unplugged. Cleaners in Screen 4 are regularly pelted with apples and sweets and one, who had spent an hour and a half cleaning it, returned to find it was once more full of litter. An apple has also appeared in the middle of the aisle even though the theatre had just been cleaned. The apple was fresh and had a single bite taken out of it.

Around the back of the complex there still remains an ancient wall and during construction work a number of bodies were found. It is thought that the area was once used as a burial site. The priory itself was burned to the ground around 1625.

Grid reference: TL06524947

Battison Street

It was reported in 'The Bedfordshire Journal' that a house in Battison Street was haunted by a ghostly couple. Mary Dorney had lived at number seven for less than a year but, even in that short time, she had seen the two ghosts several times. She described the couple as being a man, who appeared to be dressed in plus fours, and a woman, who wore a floral nightdress. The ghosts would be seen strolling around the back room of the house at night.

During the hours of daylight it is suspected that they were responsible for turning off the television set when no one was in the room. Friends and neighbours who entered the room commented on how cold and clammy the atmosphere was.

Grid reference: TL04634961

Bedford Hospital

The South Wing of Bedford Hospital has seen several instances of a supernatural nature. A nurse in 1972 was working as a trainee on Russell Ward getting the night medicines ready. As she worked she saw a young girl come up the stairs and enter the corridor. The nurse described her as being very pretty with short brown hair and rosy cheeks, wearing a long dress and long white coat. She also noted that the girl was above average height and that she was slim. The staff nurse who was just unlocking the medicine trolley also saw the girl and they both watched as she went into the toilet. They waited but she did not come out and when the trainee went to investigate she found no one there, just a very cold spot. No members of the medical or surgical staff were on duty that night and the staff nurse recalled that the figure appeared to be gliding. Later it was found out that the ghost was that of a young girl who had worked in the pathology department and who had committed suicide, at the age of twenty-three, three years previously. If the doors of Russell Ward were locked at night they would rattle as though someone was trying to enter, but when the doors were unlocked there was never anyone there.

One night, at three in the morning, the same trainee heard a shuffling sound coming from bay five of Shand Ward. About half an hour later the same sound was heard again. The trainee and the other staff nurse on duty distinctly heard the sounds of footsteps along the wall about half way between the nurses' station and bay five. They described the sounds as those that would be made by an old person, but all the patients were younger mobile men.

After a patient died, rattling sounds were heard emanating from the room he had occupied. When the room was checked, the sides of the bed were found to be down when earlier they had been up. The previous occupant had been in the habit of rattling the sides of his bed to gain attention.

Even the trainee nurse's mother had a disquieting experience whilst a patient in the hospital. As she lay in bed she felt someone get into bed with her, but there was no one there.

Grid reference: TL04764897

The Bullnose Bat

The Bullnose Bat (now refurbished and called 'The Square') in St. Paul's Square, Bedford, was the site of a gruesome discovery five years ago. At that time the pub was undergoing a major refurbishment when thirty bodies were dug up. The assistant manager remembers seeing a bottle fly across the bar of its own volition and fall into a waste bin; the event was also witnessed by the barman. The same barman also reported a phantom cat, which kept appearing in his bedroom even though the door and window were closed. A previous manager's puppy would not go near an area by the exit door where customers have reported a cold spot.

Grid reference: TL05014973

Cavendish Street

Number 36 Cavendish Street was once occupied by a drayman and his family, and by something less corporeal. The house was a new one, built about twenty years ago by the local council, on top of the foundations of a much older building. The haunted area seemed to be the top of the stairs and the stairs themselves. On numerous occasions scratching noises were heard coming from the area. At one time the sound of someone running upstairs was heard, but it could not have been a family member. The children of the family are also reported to have seen faces at the top of the stairs.

The drayman and his family, who lived at number 36, previously lived at 121B Tavistock Street (see the Tavistock Street entry herein), which they also reported as being haunted. Could the ghost have followed them to their new address?

Grid reference: TL04785047

Cecil Higgins Museum

The instances of paranormal happenings at the Cecil Higgins Museum in Bedford are almost beyond count. The most unusual place for a haunting must be the ladies' toilet. Jenny Clarke, the secretary to the Cecil Higgins Art Gallery and Museum, was washing her hands in the toilet when the door behind her suddenly slid shut. The door is a heavy one and difficult to close at the best of times and could, certainly, not have closed by itself. When you enter that particular room the air seems to grow distinctly colder.

The museum curator is always the last to leave and the first to arrive, so she was amazed to discover one morning that the ladder that she had used the night before had moved from where she had left it, so that it was now blocking the fire exit. A set of dummies which were closely packed in a display were now arranged in a straight line down the gallery.

Jenny was walking past the bottom of the stairs (a later addition to the house) when she noticed a man in a dark suit. She nodded to the man, by way of a greeting, then continued on to the kitchen. On arrival she was rather surprised to discover that the only two men in the house at the time

were already in the kitchen. Other instances involving the stairs include, a member of staff who felt they were being watched as they walked up the stairs, a young boy who felt uncomfortable and turned red in the face, and another young visitor who felt a tingling sensation when he touched the banister rail.

The drawing room is fully furnished as a tranquil Victorian setting and is well lived in, at least by the ghosts. A team from Anglia Television stayed there one night but nothing happened until the fact was mentioned, whereupon all the lights went out. This was traced to a mains switch in a closed cupboard which had mysteriously turned itself off. In addition it was found that all the security guards' batteries had been drained.

In the library the ghost of a stable boy has been seen who appears to be looking at the books. In a cabinet mirror a previous curator saw the reflection of a gentleman standing behind him, but when he turned round there was no one there. A visiting printer also saw the figure of a man sitting at a table. The security staff have also been witnesses, with one seeing a figure disappear round a corner in front of them, only to find no one there when they themselves turned the same corner and, of course, there was nowhere else for the figure to have gone.

Upstairs, in the Guest's Bedroom, is the ghost of a woman who was once seen by a visitor and her son, who both described her as wearing a blue dress with white lace trim. Many of the members of staff have felt frightened in that room but they could not say why, and they will not work up there on their own. One member of staff particularly hates the dressing table mirror.

In the Nursery visitors have seen cupboard doors close by themselves, and the pendulum from a clock once fell off, but instead of falling straight downwards, or to one side, it shot off several feet in front of the clock. One young visitor saw the pages of music on the piano turning over by themselves.

In the Hexagonal Gallery one visitor saw a bowl of oil move across the table to the edge, then rock back and forth without falling. In 1994 the portrait of Cecil Higgins fell off the wall, but the string was still found to be intact and the nail was still in place. Electrical goods have also been affected including the electric typewriter that started typing away by itself, the photocopier whose lid kept moving up and down and the old telephone system that kept making 'dialling out' noises.

The museum itself was bequeathed to the town by Cecil Higgins and is a large Victorian Mansion in Castle Close just off the river. The Gallery stands alongside the mound of Bedford Castle which saw a bloody history. In 1224 the castle was captured by Henry III after a long siege and eighty of the defenders were hung on the castle mound. It is said that, to this day, if you stand on the mound at night you can still hear the creaking of the gallows.

Grid reference: TL05274978

The Greyfriars

Danny Ward had an unusual experience outside what used to be the Greyfriars public house in Bedford. Back in the 1970s he told reporters "I saw a monk with sandals on, wearing a habit with the hood up so that you could not see his face; there was a chain around his neck and a large cross, he seemed to be looking down at the cross and meditating." The street was not empty at the time but the other people present did not seem to see the monk as they walked past him. This is not unusual as ghosts do not always appear to everyone present.

Some time later Mr. Ward remembered that the phantom friar had been seen by others. These included a girl assistant, who worked at nearby Carousel Records, who was working late when she and the other people present clearly saw the ghost.

This story is so similar to the one headed 'Allhallows' that it seems very likely that the ghosts are one and the same. Both stories happened in the 1970s and the two locations are almost the same. The only real difference between the two tales is that several people saw the ghost in the 'Allhallows' tale whilst only one man saw it in this tale, even though the ghost was walking amongst people.

Grid reference: TL04774995

The King's Arms

In the King's Arms public house in St. Mary's Street in Bedford there are reported to be two ghosts. In 1994 there was a sighting of the ghost in the cellar by an employee of the brewery. The ghost was described as a fairly old man wearing a short-sleeved white shirt. That particular ghost had a habit of throwing buckets around and it even had the ability to strip down the beer taps. After they had been cleaned and left to dry the ghost would take them apart; this according to the landlord "is no mean feat".

The second ghost has been heard upstairs in the pub. He has never been seen but he has been heard walking about. Sometimes the pub dog would bark at nothing then the floorboards would be heard creaking. Once some old nails were thrown at a customer but as there were only two people in the bar at the time they could not have done it. The nails were the type that was made by blacksmiths years ago.

Grid reference: TL05094943

Mill Street

Mill Street is said to be one of the most haunted sites in Bedford. Mr. T. B. Porter was brought up at number 38 Mill Street (now a Citizens Advice Bureau) and wrote about his experiences there to the 'Bedford Record'. Many times as a child he had heard the sound of footsteps coming from upstairs when there was no one up there. One time his mother called both himself and his brother down for dinner thinking they were upstairs, having heard the sound of footsteps, but they never responded. She found out why a little while later when they both came in from outside. The sounds she had heard upstairs were not made by them. Both his mother and the servant had been convinced that they had come inside earlier.

One time Mr. Porter's mother was alone in the house when she heard two distinct and heavy knocks on the oak back door. When she went to the door to find out who it was she discovered that there was no one there. Her husband returned shortly after and he searched the grounds but he could find no one. He told his wife that the gates to the road were securely bolted on the inside, so nobody could have gone that way.

Behind the house was a two storey coaching stables with a loft. At one point the gardener had to search the loft because of unexplained noises, but they had to remain unexplained as the loft was deserted.

In the early 1940s Mr. Porter sold the house to Bedford Corporation and it became a restaurant providing cheap meals for the duration of the

Second World War. Later it became the offices of the Corporation Housing Department, then finally the offices of the Probation Service. In 1962 the Deputy Clerk to Bedford Magistrates was working late when he heard a knock at the door. He got up to answer the knock but there was nobody there, even though he had got up promptly. Once again the knock was a heavy double knock. The room in question was situated on the first floor of the building and was allegedly the most haunted, "a gloomy room in a generally dingy building" said Derek Payne the Clerk.

Another incident involved the front door knob, which started rotating as if someone was trying to enter the room. Two witnesses were present at the time, Harry Larkworthy and John Harlow, and, even though both reached the door in two strides, they saw nothing when they opened it. A number of staff members also heard an enormous bang as if a whole load of files had been dropped along the corridor. When they investigated, there was again no one there and nothing on the floor.

Grid reference: TL05244986

Newnham Avenue

In the middle of the twentieth century at the Priory Methodist Church in Newnham Avenue a witness saw a man who appeared as if he was creeping along the back of the church. The witness was suspicious as to what the man was doing, so he continued to watch him. To his surprise the man then walked through a wall, leaving a thin wisp of smoke behind him. The witness described the man as being well dressed.

Grid reference: TL06574993

RAFA Headquarters

The Bedford Branch Headquarters of the RAF Association in Ashburnham Road is said to be haunted, by a dark figure. Numerous people have seen the ghost, which seems to haunt an area lying between the toilets, which lie to the south-east of the building, and the snooker room, which lies at the front of the building in the south-west. The ghost had been haunting the building for a number of years, but stopped about three to four years ago. At that time the building was undergoing some restructuring work upstairs and it is almost as if this had ended the haunting, which is unusual as building work is quite often the start of a haunting.

The RAFA moved into the present building in Ashburnham Road in 1977. The building was originally a large Edwardian house named Ivy Dene, which had been built by a successful Bedford plumber for his family.

Grid reference: TL04154996

Sisters House

Sisters House is a former nunnery located on St. Peters Street right next to St. Luke's church. Today it is a listed building which is currently owned and maintained by the Pilgrims Housing Association and is used

as accommodation for people with chronic mental health problems.

A number of years ago some members of staff would occasionally stay overnight while the unit was being set up. On one particular evening, in 1997, one of the staff members was asleep in one of the rooms when he was suddenly woken up by the sensation of a heavy weight on the bottom of the bed. When he switched on the light he was surprised to see the figure of a nun at the bottom of his bed. He was even more surprised when she slowly drifted down the room and passed straight through a wall. Other members of staff have said that things would go missing, but when they mentally said "Oh! Stop being silly and give it back" the items would usually reappear.

Grid reference: TL05185009

St. Peters Street

St. Peters Street in the heart of Bedford seems to be haunted by the ghost of a World War One soldier.

Keith Paull and his wife were driving down St. Peters Street in 2001 and were stopped by a red traffic light opposite the Alphonse Sandwich bar. When the light turned green they started to pull away but they didn't get very far. They were both rather surprised to see a man, dressed in an old soldiers uniform, who was crossing the road from the pavement to their left just a few yards ahead of them. The man managed to cross the road without once looking to either side and he seemed to be totally ignoring the surrounding traffic, almost as if he was completely oblivious of it. Once across the road he simply faded away into thin air. Keith and his wife described the man as being hatless and as having short hair.

Grid reference: TL05045004

Tavistock Street

A flat in Tavistock Street, number 121B, has been owned by Charles Wells brewery for a number of years, and used as accommodation by draymen. It seems that employees of the brewery have not been the only occupants, as the flat is haunted. Furniture has been known to move around and there has even been writing found on the windows of the flat. One drayman, who lived there twenty years ago, said that he would return home from work to find records playing on his record player, but there was no one there to have put them on. Numerous people, including friends of the aforementioned drayman, have stayed in the flat and reported strange feelings and happenings.

Beneath the flat there is now a café, The Tavistock Cafeteria, but about fifty years ago it was a bicycle shop where, it is said, the owner shot himself. Could he be the source of the haunting? One child, who was staying in the flat, is reported to have heard the voice of a recently deceased relative on his Fisher Price telephone; was this childish imagination, or something else?

Grid reference: TL04575035

Union Street

In Union Street, approximately one hundred metres from Bedford Prison, a dark figure has been seen. This area contains a car park so it is very popular with shoppers visiting the town centre, but two hundred years ago it was the site of a gallows. Here in 1607 a highwayman known as 'Black Tom' was hanged. He was called Black Tom because of his swarthy skin and greasy coal black hair. His body was buried at the point where Tavistock Street, Union Street and Clapham Road meet (grid reference: TL04495042) and to ensure he didn't return a stake was driven through his heart. Soon after he was buried his ghost, accompanied by another unidentified ghost, began to haunt the area. In the 1840s both ghosts were seen several times and it got so bad that nervous people would not venture out at night.

Occasionally drivers have seen a dark shape 'lurking' in the corner of the car park as they collect their cars. One witness described the figure as that of "a drunk, with his head lolling about". He soon changed his description when the figure vanished as he approached it. In 1963 several witnesses saw Black Tom in broad daylight, a figure with his face blacked staggering along Union Street with his head lolling to one side in a gruesome fashion. This was the last reported sighting.

This was the story as I heard it, but a couple of aspects require some clarification. Firstly, there is no car park in Union Street; well that is not strictly true as there is one, but it is solely for the use of people visiting the health clinic and not for shoppers. There is metered parking along the road, but it is quite a walk from there to the town centre. In fact Union Street is more like three hundred metres from Bedford Prison (a very approximate one hundred metres). The nearest real car park is in Greyfriars, which lies roughly south of the prison and conveniently about one hundred metres away. But was there a car park in Union Street forty years ago? And if there was a car park in Union Street, where exactly was it located?

Grid reference: TL044502

BEESTON

The village of Beeston lies on either side of the very busy A1 just south of Sandy. Half of the houses in the village, including the village pub, face towards the A1. The other half of the village faces in towards a large square green which is a registered common and therefore can never be developed.

The Cross

The most recent haunting incident that has occurred at the Cross was in response to a group of sceptics. After categorically stating that ghosts didn't exist, the chalk on the pool table, where they were playing, suddenly rose into the air. Sometime later a bottle of whisky fell off the shelf for no reason and smashed. After that they were not so sceptical.

Other happenings have included the beer gas turning itself off and the lager line has somehow managed to revert to the empty barrel just after it had been changed. One Sunday night shortly after new owners took over the pub they found that no one had come in for a drink. They found out why when they realised the customers were waiting in the car park. The doors were now locked and bolted and the key was behind the bar but they had been opened just a little while before. In another incident two women got trapped in the toilet when the doors were inexplicably locked after they had gone inside.

Sylvia, the landlady, feels that the ghost is a mischievous one and not malevolent and she gets the feeling that she is being watched when she is in the cellar, almost as if the ghost is checking that she is doing things right. The previous owners warned the new owners about the ghost; at first they weren't convinced, now they are.

Grid reference: TL16884834

BLETSOE

The village of Bletsoe is relatively small with a population of only 210. It lies just under ten kilometres to the north of Bedford and consists of rows of estate cottages and more modern houses around the triangular village green. Unlike most villages the present day population is less than it was in the 1600s.

The mother of Henry VII, Lady Margaret Beaufort, lived in the village; it was also the seat of Oliver St. John who was Parliamentary leader during the English Civil War. He was one of the signatories to Charles I's death warrant.

Bletsoe Castle is the remains of a mansion built in the sixteenth century by the St. John family. To the north-west of the village the remains have been found of a Saxon burial site and Roman buildings.

The Falcon Inn

Steve Elliott took over management of the inn in October 1995 and things started to happen almost straight away. A pair of bookshelves was seen to fall from the wall then float across the room, and strange footsteps were heard. Several people heard the footsteps, but when they all rushed upstairs to see who it was there was no one there.

The poltergeist activity seemed to increase when Steve had a girlfriend and one even had bottles, books and glasses thrown at her. Items also went missing, only to reappear several days later. Steve also heard several voices all whispering at once, so he felt that there may have been more than one ghost present. The events became so interesting that the 'Bedford and Kempston Herald' carried a report in June 1996.

In the old stables (which are now used as a bottle store) of the sixteenth century inn it is said that you get a very strong feeling that you are being watched, but the observer is never seen.

One previous resident of the inn, who stayed there for five months, said that there is a corridor upstairs at the back of the building where the sound of a very heavy footed person walking up and down can be heard. He also reported that he had seen the feet of this person underneath his bedroom door, but there was never anyone there when the door was opened. In addition the loud screams of a baby in pain have been heard.

These were heard whilst the resident and others were staying in a bedroom at the back of the house. This crying would only happen once or twice every two to three months and was even heard by the Head Chef.

At the front of the building one bedroom was occupied by the Dessert Chef. She would leave her room in an untidy state (clothes all over the place), only to return and find that it had been tidied. This was witnessed twice by the aforementioned resident who saw her lock the door when they left, yet all was neat and tidy when they returned. Clothes had been placed neatly on the bed, and the woman's shoes were placed in pairs alongside the bed. There was no other way to access the room apart from through the door, and the Dessert Chef had the only key. The witness saw this happen twice in a period of five months.

Around the end of the 1700s an ostler, who was working at the inn, met with an unfortunate accident. According to legend, he was found dead having fallen from the hayloft. Now, it would seem, his ghost returns to haunt the inn. He has been seen in the grounds of the inn, as well as in the inn itself, especially the kitchens.

Grid reference: TL01815788

BOLNHURST

Bolnhurst is closely aligned with Keysoe and consists of a number of dwellings dotted along the side of the Bedford to Kimbolton Road with a total population of 710 people.

The area mainly consists of farmsteads and timber framed cottages in amongst north Bedfordshire's rolling countryside. Bolnhurst has its own parish church, St. Dunstan's, peeping out from an area of trees.

Ye Olde Plough

The ghost which haunts 'Ye Olde Plough' was one who was felt as opposed to being seen or heard. Several people have felt his presence and one, who was staying the night, felt the bed dip as if someone had sat on the mattress. The pub was eventually closed, as it was unprofitable, and converted into a spiritual centre. Later this closed and the building was once more put up for sale (sold as of early January 2005).

The original building, dating back to around 1480, was a farmhouse called 'Brayes', part of the manor of Backenho. By 1538 it was in the possession of John Francklyn of Thurleigh and it remained in his family until 1640 when it passed to John and William Halsey. In 1665 the Great Plague struck the village and it was razed to the ground, but Brayes survived as it was outside the contaminated area.

Grid reference: TL08765867

CARDINGTON

Cardington lies five kilometres south-east of Bedford and has a population of 290. The village consists of estate cottages clustered around the village green. Many of the cottages in the village bear the initials 'JH' or 'SW'.

SW relates to Samuel Whitbread, the brewer, who was born at Maltings Farm, which is the red bricked building to the west of the green.

JH stands for John Howard who was one of the first prison reformers and after whom the Howard League for Penal Reform is named (founded in 1866). He used to live in the white washed Georgian house which lies to the north of the church.

Cardington is most famous for the airship hangers at Shortstown and the fate of the R101. The bodies of the men who died in the airship disaster are buried in the small cemetery at Cardington.

Airship Hangers

The old airship hangers at Cardington aren't actually haunted but people still feel that they are an unlucky place.

On 4th October 1930 the great airship, the R101, slipped her moorings for a flight to Karachi over six thousand kilometres away. This was the start of an ill-fated journey that would culminate in disaster and the death of forty-eight passengers and crew members leaving just six

survivors. The flight had been brought forward by the then Secretary of State for Air, Lord Thomson. He wanted to fly to India and back in time to make a grand entrance to the Imperial Conference of Dominion Prime Ministers in October. Because of this the airship was launched before she was really ready. As it took off it couldn't gain any altitude so the Captain had to order four tons of water ballast, half the total, to be dropped. The airship managed to cross the channel through heavy rain which increased her weight, forcing her down dangerously close to the waves.

Just after crossing Beauvais at two o'clock in the morning the airship hit a hummock of earth and burst into flames. One eyewitness said that she had barely cleared Beauvais church steeple. As the airship was filled with over fifty thousand cubic metres (fifty million litres) of hydrogen, the temperature was enough to melt her metal superstructure, and the only people to survive were five engineering members of the crew and a wireless operator.

The strange aspect of the tale occurred two days later when a séance was held at the National Laboratory of Psychical Research in London. The medium, Eileen Garrett, seemed to make contact with the Captain, Flight Lieutenant H. Carmichael Irwin. Some of his first words were "Never mind about me, but do for heaven's sake give this to them." Eileen then rattled off a whole series of details which were taken in shorthand. The technical data which Eileen related regarded things of which she would not have had any prior knowledge and which included mention of future experiments that Irwin was aware of but Eileen could never have known. When the details were given to an expert at the Royal Airship Works at Cardington he agreed that they were correct in almost every detail. During the séance Irwin had said that the airship had "scraped the roofs at Achy" but no one knew where that was until a large scale railway map of France revealed Achy as a small village on the route that the R101 would have taken to Beauvais.

You get a very good view of the airship hangers from the A600 just to the south of Shortstown (grid reference: TL07674673). The island at this point on the A600 has a left turn (when coming from Shortstown) into a dead end, with the hangers located just a few hundred metres across the fields to the east.

The memorial is in the graveyard at Cardington. This can be found on the right as you approach the village from the A421(T) about one hundred metres before the church (grid reference: TL08524798). When I first saw the memorial I was understandably taken aback when I discovered that the first name on the side of the memorial was my own name, William H. King (on the right hand side as seen in the picture on the previous page). This poor victim of the disaster was a member of the crew and an engineer. Even though my family have named their first born son William H. King for generations (I was the first to break the tradition) he was, in fact, not related to my family.

Even though the hangers are not haunted, several local people have reported that their homes are. The ghosts are said to be those of members of the R101 crew who have returned to search for their loved ones.

Grid reference: TL081468

CHELLINGTON

Chellington and Carlton were at one time separate villages but are now effectively joined with a combined population of 840. They share a common street which runs down to Harrold Bridge, a raised mediaeval causeway that provided a dry route during times of flood. It was the building of the causeway which united the villages. Even after the villages were joined their origins were still marked by the original parish churches, St. Mary's to the west and St. Nicholas to the east.

Carlton Hill

The ancient road which runs from Chellington to Pavenham rises up forty-five metres from the valley as Carlton Hill. A lady cyclist from

Harrold was pushing her bicycle up Carlton Hill when she observed two horses which were galloping at speed straight towards her. For her own safety she moved out of the way onto the grass verge as the horses went thundering past. At the speed they were travelling she feared there would be a terrible accident when they reached the crossroads in the centre of Chellington (grid reference: SP95705579), so she cycled quickly back down the hill to see if she could help. When she reached the crossroads she found that there was no sign of the horses.

In more recent times motorists have had to brake sharply on Carlton Hill when they were confronted with a galloping phantom horse and rider.

Grid reference: SP960555

CHICKSANDS

The most prominent feature of Chicksands is the priory built for the Gilbertine order that was the only monastic order to have been created in England. They were unusual in that monks and nuns lived in mixed houses and not separated as was usually the case. Parts of the priory were incorporated into the existing house built by the Osborn family shortly after the Dissolution in the early 1500s.

In 1950 Chicksands became a communication base for the United States Air Force. It is now occupied by the Defence Intelligence and Security Centre.

Chicksands Priory

The haunting of Chicksands Priory dates back to before the dissolution of the monasteries and is believed to be due to Berta Rosata, a sixteenth century nun. In 1535 Thomas Cromwell received a report from Doctor Richard Layton concerning the priory. This report stated that two of the nuns were pregnant, one by a servant and the other by a canon. One of these nuns, Berta Rosata, was walled up in the priory for her sins but not before she was made to witness the beheading of her lover. It is thought that the haunting is Berta seeking the body of her lover.

Descriptions of the ghost, who appears on the seventeenth of each month, vary from a woman wearing white with a white train flowing behind her to a nun in normal vestments. She has been reported as having long black hair which covered her face. Descriptions from the American and British officers staying at Chicksands and numerous civilians have been so varied that it is possible that there are three or even four female ghosts haunting the site.

The legend was given further credence when a plaque was found in the only surviving cloister bearing the inscription:

Moribus Ornata Jacet Hic Bona Berta Rosata

This roughly translates as 'By Virtues guarded and by manners graced, here alas is fair Rosata placed'. The punishment does seem a little harsh even by mediaeval standards and no trace of fair Rosata was found when the wall was rebuilt in the eighteenth and nineteenth centuries. It is worthy of note that the plaque isn't actually on a cloister wall as was claimed but is in fact on the wall of what would have been the cellar. In fact it transpires that the plaque appears to be an invention of the eighteenth century. One question, because of the change from the Julian to the Gregorian calendar in 1582, which effectively moved a date in the 1500s by ten days, did Rosata originally appear on the seventh of the month and not the seventeenth as she always does now?

During the First World War a maid, who had been working at the Priory for thirty years, was taking a glass of milk to the King James's Room. It was ten o'clock on a winter's evening when, in dim light, she saw a "tall fascinating woman dressed in white" who moved rapidly past her whilst she was in the picture gallery. Again during WW1 a man was found dead outside the priory. His hair had turned white overnight and his face was found to be frozen into a look of abject terror. It is said that he died of fright.

During the Second World War an RAF officer decided to play a joke based on the legend and dressed up in an old sheet. He stood outside the King James's Room and managed to scare some poor unsuspecting girl.

44

When another person turned up in response to the girls scream the man fled and he ran straight into a real ghost, which he described as a woman in black with dishevelled hair partly covering a wrinkled face. The ghost then promptly disappeared through the wall, leaving the man feeling as if he had been visited by a case of poetic justice.

In the 1950s George Inskip, who had been head gardener at the priory for thirty years, was working in the greenhouse when he saw "a dark, greyish shape" coming up the path. When he went outside there was no one there. In 1957 an RAF Lieutenant was violently clawed on his left side while sleeping in the officers' quarters. He was dragged in the direction of the clawing by the ghost, who he reported as having "an intensely illuminated youthful face". The ghost smiled at him "in the most friendly and intimate manner", then disappeared into a pinpoint of light with a hollow ringing howl. It didn't end there because, when the officer worked up the courage to check the room, he saw the motionless head and shoulders of a woman wearing a nun's headdress. She stared straight past him then slowly faded away. Any doubts he had were dispelled the next day when he found his side covered in bruises. Three years earlier another RAF officer had seen "a ruddy faced woman with untidy hair, holding a notepad, wearing a dark dress with lace collar" at the foot of his bed.

One very interesting story concerns an airman who was cycling by the priory when he saw a ghost. He was shaken by the event but his wife dismissed his story as having been influenced by drink. The following February he met the apparition again. The ghost came from the direction of the river and walked up to the building in the south-east corner, then promptly rose up and disappeared into the second floor. On a print of the priory from 1730 an external staircase is clearly shown in the south-east corner of the building but the airman would never have known this.

Chicksands Priory was originally built by the Countess Rohese and dates back to 1150. Later it was to become the third largest house of the Gilbertine order, accommodating nearly one hundred monks and nuns. When the Abbey was dissolved in October 1538 there were only twenty three people living there. Since then the house has had several owners including Sir Peter Osborn who occupied it from 1540 to 1587. The house remained in the hands of the Osborn family until they sold it to the Government in 1936. In 1946 the building was taken over by the RAF who used it as an officers' mess.

It is said that a tunnel ran from the priory to the town, but it was sealed as 'something' kept violently attacking visitors.

Grid reference: TL12113930

Chicksands Wood

In 1971 a motorist who was driving through Chicksands Wood was somewhat unnerved when he came face to face with a ghost. What made it doubly unnerving for the poor motorist was the fact that the apparition was mounted on a horse which he promptly rode straight through the man's car!

The wood lies, fairly literally, in the middle of nowhere and there are no macadamised roads going through it. Along the spine of the wood there is a reasonably wide track (Long Drive) made of compacted stones, which would certainly support a car, so on that basis it is possible that someone was driving down it, but how long have the stones been there? If the stones are recent (the track isn't as it appears on the 1892 map of the wood) then it would have been a dirt road. Chicksands Wood lies just a few hundred metres from Northfield Farm, near which a phantom horse and rider has been seen (see the Clophill: Great Lane section). Could the Great Lane and Chicksands Wood apparitions be the same ghost on the way to Chicksands Priory?

The path through the wood is no longer accessible to unauthorised vehicles but makes for a pleasant walk. It is best reached from Appley Corner (grid reference: TL10614109), which lies at the north end of the wood just over one kilometre from the A600. Unfortunately the shortest road from the A600 to Appley Corner crosses a bridge one hundred metres from the wood. I say unfortunately because the bridge is currently closed (unsafe – early 2005). The only other route is to take the Northwood End Road into Haynes, if you are travelling north-west along the A600, or come off the A600 just north of Haynes and follow the Silver End Road into Haynes. From the centre of Haynes follow Plummers Lane south until you reach Church End Road (grid reference: TL09724138), then turn east to Appley Corner.

Grid reference: TL101403

CHILTERN GREEN

Chiltern Green Road

One night, at the beginning of the 1900s, a pedestrian was walking along the road between Chiltern Green and the railway station which used to exist at New Mill End (along Chiltern Green Road), when he saw a light approaching in the distance. Thinking it was a bicycle, he moved to one side to allow it to pass and was very surprised when the light suddenly veered off to one side and went straight through a hedgerow. A letter appeared in the 'Herts Advertiser' of the time telling of the strange white light which had appeared near where the body of a suicide had been found.

Grid reference: TL130186

CHURCH END

Church End is an isolated hamlet one kilometre north of Kensworth. It sits in a valley and consists of a few houses and farms, and the church of St. Mary the Virgin. The church is the only one in the area, so that parishioners from Kensworth had to walk along the narrow Hollick's Lane or across the fields, into and out of a steep valley, to reach their place of worship.

The area in which the twelfth century church stands was the original centre of Kensworth, until the enclosures of the eighteenth century forced people to build their houses adjacent to Kensworth Common, the only available public grazing area. The remains of a Saxon church have been found on the site, showing that Church End has had religious connections predating the Norman conquest of 1066.

Headless Milkmaid

The church of St. Mary the Virgin at Church End, Kensworth and a nearby footpath, which runs north from the churchyard, are haunted by a headless spirit.

The ghost appears to be a milkmaid, complete with yoke from which hang two pails. Her most striking feature is her singular lack of a head! She walks down the path coming from the direction of the woods to the north and enters the churchyard. There are three local legends as to the origin of the ghost. The first has it that she was waylaid and murdered as she walked down the path. The second version of her death claims that she was killed by farm machinery in the early nineteenth century. In the third legend she dies a natural death, then her lover takes her head so that part of her can remain with him forever.

The footpath can be accessed via a stile on the north boundary of the churchyard (grid reference: TL03111905), or from the narrow Beech

Road, which runs from Dunstable to Church End, three hundred and fifty metres to the north (grid reference: TL03121938). From the road the path drops down a gentle slope, past a wood on the right, towards the church.

Footpath Number 4 from Kensworth to Church End is also haunted by a headless milkmaid but there are no specific details. Could this, again, be a case of the location being incorrectly given, or does this spirit haunt both paths?

Grid reference: TL031190

Incorporeal Witch

The footpath which runs from Beech Road, to the north of Church End, towards the church is haunted by the ghost of a witch. The ghost is said to be that of an old woman, wearing a black four cornered hat, which would date her to the late eighteenth century.

She follows the path from the woods, which lie three hundred metres to the north of the church, until she reaches the stile into the churchyard (grid reference: TL03111905), but there she stops. Instead of entering the churchyard she angrily shakes her fist at the church. Legend has it that a local witch was forbidden to enter the churchyard and now she spends eternity venting her anger at the church.

Footpath Number 4 from Kensworth to Church End is also said to be haunted by a witch but there are no descriptions of her. Could it just be that the location of the haunting (most likely in the Kensworth case) has been misplaced or does the witch haunt both paths?

Grid reference: TL031190

CLOPHILL

Clophill lies in a heavily wooded area with the village running east off the A6 Luton to Bedford road. The population is currently 1,810.

The Flying Horse pub was a very important coaching inn and legend has it that Dick Turpin stopped there on his ride to York.

The village once had a reputation for the excellence of its straw plaiting. At the west end of the High Street is the village lockup and pound. The village itself contains several old houses and walls built of mellow stone. On a ridge above the village stands the ruin of St. Mary's church which is now a designated Ancient Monument and which has a gruesome past.

South-east of the village, just off the Shefford Road (A507), lies the earthworks of Cainhoe Castle, which dates from Norman times.

Great Lane

Just after Christmas 1969 a newsagent and his wife were delivering papers to Northfield Farm (grid reference: TL08954002), when they saw a small light approaching along the Haynes Church End to Clophill road (Great Lane). Believing it to be a cyclist, the driver dipped his headlights and slowed down, only to discover that it was actually a rider on horseback carrying a lantern. To avoid frightening the horse the driver stopped the car and turned off the lights. As the rider approached they could clearly see that the man was hooded like a monk. Without stopping, the horse and rider passed, literally, straight through the car, much to the surprise of the occupants.

They did not mention the event to anybody, but a year later a lady asked the newsagent if he had ever met a cloaked figure on horseback during his early morning deliveries. It transpired that the lady used to live at Northfield Cottage (grid reference: TL08823978) at the start of the road to Northfield Farm but had moved as the family were too upset by the ghost.

A farmer in Haynes was found to own a similar lantern to the one the ghost had carried and which was over two hundred years old. The newsagent believes that the ghost was on his way to the nearby Chicksands Priory, as it is said that there used to be a path to the priory which paralleled Northfield Farm's driveway.

Near to Northfield Farm lies Chicksands Wood which is said to be haunted by a rider on horseback (see the Chicksands Wood entry herein).

Could this be the same horse and rider as the one seen on Great Lane? The present path through the woods is not on a direct line from Northfields Farm to Chicksands Priory, but it does cross the direct route, about half way along the former's length.

Grid reference: TL086399

St. Mary's Church

St. Mary's and the churchyard are now a ruin which has had a grisly past. During the 1960s it was twice used for what were purported to be black magic rituals. In March 1963 the grave of the wife of an eighteenth century apothecary, Jenny Humberstone, was opened and her bones were later found in the nave of the church, arranged in what appeared to be a ritualistic pattern. The bones formed a circle with cockerel feathers placed nearby and her skull was found impaled on a railing. The bones were

eventually reburied in her original grave by the church porch. In 1969, on Midsummer's Eve, graves were again broken into and bones removed. No clue has ever been found as to the people who did this, but it seems likely that the Black Mass was involved as the sixties were a time of occult revival with many groups being interested in the darker aspects. In 1975 bones were again removed from the graves, but this time they were just scattered around the site so this may, therefore, have been the work of vandals.

Local inhabitants believe that the site is haunted by 'Sophie's Ghost', especially when a visitor and his wife photographed the church and discovered a figure in the church window clad in white and looking down the church nave. The strangeness was heightened when they realised that the window lies nearly two metres above the nave floor, though this would correspond with the height of the pulpit.

The site is a very apt one for the diabolic purposes to which it was put. The church itself is located on the top of a hill a good half a kilometre from the nearest habitation and is reached by a narrow, potholed, unmetallised lane called Old Church Path (grid reference: TL09263823, seven hundred metres from the Shefford Road). An alternative route to the church is to park along Great Lane, six hundred and fifty metres along from the junction with the High Street (grid reference: TL08963875). Parking is difficult in that area, but there are a couple of places to partially pull off the narrow road. From there you walk along the Greensand Ridge Path, heading east for about two hundred and fifty metres.

The area has a very strange atmosphere what with the ruin and the location coupled with the knowledge of what has happened there. The church itself is unusual as the tower lies to the east end of the church instead of the normal west. Most people say that the church is the wrong way round but this is not the case. The important main window still faces east so that the congregation face the light, the rising sun, and not into the dark, the setting sun. This has resulted in the window being placed in the tower. The hill on which the church stands is invariably referred to as Deadman's Hill, but this actually lies nearly two kilometres away to the west (on the A6) across a wide valley. Deadman's Hill is where James Hanratty was said to have murdered Michael Gregson in 1961.

Another unusual aspect of the church is the fact that there are no grave markers near the church. Instead they have all been moved to the north and south boundaries of the site. This was probably brought about due to the previously recorded ritualistic events, in an attempt to hide the true locations of the graves so that they couldn't be attacked again. To the west there are graves still in their original positions (many lying in amongst the trees and bushes) and a more modern graveyard to the north.

The present building was constructed in the fifteenth century but there has been a church on the site for at least the last eight hundred and fifty years. Prior to this the hill was used as the site for a leper colony. In the church some of the original mediaeval lime plaster still survives in which, it is said, can be seen the original consecration crosses, though I have not managed to spot them. The church has two very large perpendicular windows to the north and south of the nave. The church now sits on its own due to the Great Plague of 1665 when the surrounding village was burnt to the ground.

Clophill has two churches, with the second, Victorian, church lying down the valley in the village. Because of the close proximity of the second church to the village and the long walk up to St. Mary's on the hill, it was decided to decommission the latter church in the late 1950s. Bedfordshire County Council purchased the site in 1977 after the church was declared redundant in 1972 and it is now a Scheduled Monument. Maintenance work continues and recently some of the overgrown areas of the cemetery were being tidied up and the trees cut back.

Grid reference: TL09183885

Site Report

I have visited St. Mary's church ruin at Clophill numerous times. My first visit was made as part of my first outing with The Luton Paranormal Society in February 2004. Twice I have parked at the top of Old Church Path next to the church and once I parked along Great

Lane and walked to the church along the Greensand Ridge path. Two of the visits were after midnight and the other was at eleven in the evening.

Despite its reputation I did not find the site creepy but it is in an excellent location, remote and dark atop a hill. The worst aspect of the site is the graffiti which covers the church and the damage which has been done to the mediaeval plaster work.

The site has such a reputation that teenagers will turn up there at night with the purpose of scaring themselves. During a recent visit, accompanied by my daughter, I observed two car loads of teenagers who arrived at midnight on a wet and windy night, but only one of them was brave enough to leave the cars. We hid twenty metres away and listened, hoping they would leave, but they stayed with the car headlights illuminating the church in an attempt to dispel the dark. After fifteen minutes we decided we were going in and walked straight past the cars onto the site, much to the consternation of the occupants. When we walked into the nave we heard "God, they're going in!" Even though they had travelled some way to get to the church, they would not follow us in, though they did turn off the headlights after a while (we felt that they did this for our sake). The reputation of the site certainly affects peoples thinking; they claimed they didn't believe in ghosts but they still wouldn't go inside. As we left, one of the occupants of the cars said "did you see those flashing lights?" and they were obviously shocked, though the lights in question were caused by the flash on our camera. Halloween is the worst, with virtual gangs turning up to 'scare' themselves, making the site a place to avoid (anyway, nothing is going to happen with that many people around).

COPLE

Cople is a small village with a population of 720, lying just less than two kilometres to the east of Cardington.

The parish church of All Saints is famous for its collection of monumental brasses which are the best in the county. To the north-west of the church stands the picturesque former nineteenth century Parish Bier House, now in the grounds of a private residence.

The Five Bells

In the corner by the fireplace in the Five Bells sits the ghost of a sailor. He has been described as a matelot, though the connection with the sea may be due to the fact that the oak beams in the building were, erroneously, thought to have originally come from Elizabethan ships. Descriptions of the figure always agree that he is old but of indefinable age, that he has his hair tied in a pigtail, that he wears a hooped shirt, that he has puttees around his lower legs and that he smokes a clay pipe. He sits in a pew which is a common feature in the public house. A previous landlady, Kate Henderson, saw him several times during her twenty-three year tenancy. The most recent sighting of the ghost has been within the last few years.

The building which the Five Bells occupies originally dates from 1690 and it had its first licence granted in 1729 to Eliza Smith. The name was originally chosen as the church opposite had five bells. Today the church has six bells but the pub name has remained unchanged.

Grid reference: TL10374844

CRANFIELD

Cranfield lies to the west of the county and has a population of 5,220. The village was once famed for its lace making but now its fame lies in Cranfield University, one of UK industry's leading post-graduate research and development centres. Cranfield is also known for its airport which is one of the busiest general aviation airfields in the country.

Marston Hill

Some thirty years ago Terry Bush and an unidentified accomplice were cycling back to Flitwick and reported "It was very late and we'd had a few and it was one of those clear moonless nights. We were at the bottom of Marston Hill when we suddenly ceased our chatter and accelerated our bikes to the junction of Horsepool Lane. There we stopped to catch our breath and both said simultaneously 'Did you see it too?'"

At the bottom of Marston hill they had spotted a figure moving towards them up the hill. They reported that the figure was headless and dressed in black with a white front. Thirty years later, Terry had a different theory to that of a ghostly sighting. "It could have been a man with his coat over his head 'cos it was so cold that night, or a giant penguin and for a more realistic guess, a Friesian cow...we just spooked and accelerated away."

Grid reference: SP972428

Wood End Road

A legend tells of a rider, Lady Snagge, who was waylaid by thieves on the Wood End Road in Cranfield which resulted in her death. She was riding along the road to meet her lover and ran into a rope that the thieves had tied across the road to dislodge any passing riders. Unfortunately the speed at which she was travelling, coupled with her failure to spot the rope, resulted in her being decapitated. The thieves, with little regard for what they had just done, quickly stripped the body of its fine clothes and jewellery before fleeing.

Over the centuries, Lady Snagge's ghost has been felt riding along the lane, either in search of her murderers or completing the journey she started in life. In the church of St. Mary the Virgin in Marston Moretaine you can see the red veined alabaster tomb with a monument to the memory of Thomas Snagge and his wife Elizabeth.

Lady Snagge's husband was an elected Member of Parliament, a barrister, Attorney General for Ireland and the elected Speaker to the House of Commons in the late sixteenth century. Elizabeth was the mother of five sons and two daughters and outlived her husband by some forty-three years and possibly spent the last years of her life in Cranfield. Thomas Snagge's last will and testament of 1591 states "I bequeath also to my said wyfe during the saide term if she liveth so long, my conduitt and hoppe in Cranfield in the County of Bedfordshire and my lane called Venison Lane in Cranfield."

At the time of her death Lady Elizabeth Snagge would have been in her eighties, so the tale of a lover seems unlikely. But Elizabeth was not the only Lady Snagge who could have been a candidate for the ghost.

Elizabeth was followed by Anne (or Anna) whose husband Thomas (most of the Lord Snagges were named Thomas) died in 1675. She was followed by Dorothy whose husband died in 1687 and Mary who married Edward Snagge in the late seventeenth century. Any one of these could have had a lover at Brogborough Park where the Wood End Road leads across the fields.

Mary Street wrote about the ghost in her book on Cranfield. She said that it materialised along the Wood End Road where there used to be an avenue of trees running from the road that was known as Lady Snagge's Walk. In the mid nineteenth century the local Rector exorcised the ghost with 'bell, book, and candle'. Doris Malsher suggested that Lady Snagge rode a powerful horse in the dark and was invisible, but those affected by her presence could feel the swish of the animal as it galloped past and on to the Round House at Brogborough Park (at grid reference: SP96943850).

Grid reference: SP956412

DUNSTABLE

Dunstable grew up as a small settlement named *Durocobrivis*, where the ancient Icknield Way and the Roman road Watling Street met. In Saxon times the settlement was abandoned until Dunstable was established by Henry I as a new market town. Henry granted the town to the Augustinian priory that he had established there in 1131.

Dunstable became a town of considerable importance, with regular royal visits complete with jousting tournaments which took place at the foot of Blow's Down. The Priory was the location from which Cranmer announced the annulment of Henry VIII's marriage to Katherine of Aragon in 1533. Dunstable continued to be important until the Priory was dissolved in the sixteenth century. Part of the original priory structure can now be seen as the Priory Church.

Watling Street was an important stagecoach route, from London to the north, which brought a great deal of wealth to the town, with at least two of the former coaching inns still surviving. Present day population is 33,110.

The Black Horse

The Black Horse public house stood on the north side of West Street, but it has now gone. When it was open, things had a habit of moving themselves from the place where you left them. In the cellar, if you put something down, the lights would go off, and by the time they came back on the object had moved.

Tidying up the bar at night became somewhat of a waste of time, because by the morning everything would be found in disarray. One barmaid reported seeing the ghost of a man quietly sitting in the bar; she said that he appeared to be dressed like a Roundhead from the Civil War.

There was one aspect of the man which absolutely convinced her that he was a ghost...his lack of a head.

Grid reference: TL018218

Buttercup Lane

Dunstable's strangest 'ghost' story must come from Buttercup Lane. In March 1969 two men, Martin Leach and Richard Wright, were walking along a narrow footpath (the Icknield Way) that leads from Canesworde Road onto the Dunstable Downs. They suddenly saw something which Martin later described. "It was white at first, then it turned black, it had a big hat, like a trilby, and glided about eighteen inches off the ground, it didn't have features like a person, it was about eight to ten feet tall and very broad." Robert added his own comments. "It didn't have any arms or legs but was wearing a large hat and it floated rather than moved."

The footpath is reached by following Buttercup Lane which comes off Canesworde Road as the latter turns to the south-east just after Meadway, if you are coming from the direction of Dunstable town centre (grid reference: TL01282096). Buttercup Lane goes gently uphill then turns left through a gateway, where it continues as a private road. At this point the path can be seen on the right (grid reference: TL01242082), still following the line of Buttercup Lane.

Grid reference: TL011205

Buttertons

Buttertons, in Middle Row on High Street South, is like a lot of shops in that area, in that it occupies an old building which has two entrances, one on the High Street and the second in Ashton Square. Like a lot of old buildings this one has a resident ghost which has not been seen but has been heard. The ghost is heard walking up and down the stairs; though, from the sound, it is felt that there could be more than one ghost.

Grid reference: TL01922178

Church Walk

Church Walk is a narrow footpath that runs from the High Street towards the Priory Church. It was once known as Corpse Walk, as it was the route by which coffins would be taken to the Priory Church. Fifty years ago the path, which runs between buildings, was very dark, only being lit by a couple of feeble gas lamps, and most people would avoid using it if they could.

In the late 40s Reuben, a resident of Dunstable, was walking from the Saracen's Head public house, in High Street South, to the Royal Oak, which used to be in Church Street, just after Kingsway. He decided to cut the corner by walking down Church Walk, thinking it would be alright, as he was accompanied by his large, black dog named Satan.

As they walked down the path Satan ran off in front, until he reached a point at the end of the buildings, whereupon he stood rooted to the spot staring towards the church. He began to snarl and bare his teeth, and his hackles rose, but Reuben could not work out why, as he couldn't see anything. Suddenly the dog gave out a yelp and fled back down the alley, past Reuben, and into the High Street where, unfortunately, he was killed by a passing car. At no time could Reuben see anything, and what had spooked the poor dog was never discovered.

Grid reference: TL01992186

Monastic Ghost

There were once two monasteries in Dunstable. The first lay to the south of the present Priory Church and a second was discovered opposite the gates to Priory Gardens, near the area now occupied by Ashton Square. An archaeological excavation was undertaken which was overseen by a County Archaeologist from Bedford who stayed in a caravan on the site.

One night, about one in the morning, the archaeologist was woken from his sleep by the caravan shaking. He got out of bed and looked outside, but he could see nothing. The caravan continued to shake, so he went outside to investigate. As he walked round to the back of the caravan he came face to face with a hooded monk wearing the black habit of the Benedictine's (who had once occupied the monastery). The archaeologist fled to the safety of the caravan and stayed inside for the rest of the night. The following morning he left Dunstable and it is said that he has never returned.

Grid reference: TL020216

Moon Wolf

Number 14 in West Street, is occupied by a New Age shop called Moon Wolf, and by the ghost of a man named George. It seems that George is carrying on from where he left off in life, as George is a flirtatious ghost. He is definitely attracted to any female visitors to the premises and has made himself felt in several ways; he has also been seen on more than one occasion. When the shop was first opened, about four years ago, the female owners became aware of George very soon after they moved in. It seems that he would comb their hair, or pull it, and was even known to sit in their laps.

The owners hold workshops in a room at the back of the building, on the upper floor, and it is here that George is most active. Once he was seen by two women attending a workshop; one lady refused to return to the building as a result (the other ended up working there). The room in which George has appeared has a couple of heaters to warm it up, but visitors have had to wear hats and coats as the room is ice cold, so much so that some have literally turned blue. Once George appeared on the instructor, Jane's, lap, making faces at one of the other women present. Jane couldn't see him, but the other woman could. One of the employees, Claire, is a medium who has seen George and has talked to him. She had drawn a picture of

George as a result of her contact with him; this image is reproduced on the previous page. When she showed it to the woman she said that it was the man she had seen.

George is definitely a ladies man, as he is never around if there are just men in the building, but he is always around when there are women. It seems he is also a jealous ghost. One day there were four women in the building, and one man who was actively flirting with them. All of a sudden, the whole building shook and the covers fell off the light fittings. Everyone rushed outside, fearing that a lorry had hit the building, but there was nothing there. Was it George making his presence felt because of the other man?

Claire, the medium, learned a lot from George, which was confirmed by local research. It seems that George was staying in the building when it was once an inn. He was engaged to a woman who was living in London and he was supposed to be travelling up there by coach, but he was late. In his haste, he rushed out of the building and was crushed beneath the wheels of another coach. He was still alive, so he was brought into the inn and put into the upper room at the back of the building, the one he now haunts. His injuries were mortal, broken limbs and internal bleeding, and eventually he succumbed to them.

One other event, that was attributed to this haunting, happened just over a year ago in the late autumn. A class was being run, in the upper front room of the building, when suddenly the four or five people present heard the sounds of neighing horses outside. They all rushed to the window to peer out, but there was nothing there. After this, George disappeared for a year, but he has now returned. Jane feels that he went home for a while.

George isn't the only ghost in the building, as another has been seen on the upper landing. At the head of the stairs is a room, which was also used for teaching sessions, but Jane always felt 'strange' when she was there. Things got so bad that she even passed out, something she had never done before, or since. A baby has been heard crying there, and the ghosts of a mother and baby have been seen on the stairs.

The building is an old one dating back to the 1400s, though its origins go back further, as there is part of a Roman wall in the cellar. In the 1600s it was an inn with stables out the back. Sometime after the inn closed, the building was divided into two, one half of which Moon Wolf now occupies. It is even said that there is a body buried in the cellar.

Grid reference: TL01822184

Nationwide

The Nationwide Building Society occupies number twenty on High Street North and is the home of the White Lady. She has been seen several times walking around the upper floors, but no one knows who she is or why she haunts that particular building.

Grid reference: TL01852189

The Packhorse Inn

On a Sunday morning in 1973 a taxi driver was on his way to collect a fare and was passing a spot near the Packhorse Inn on the A5 when he received a sudden fright. A tall man, reported to be about six feet tall, wearing white clothes, stepped right in front of the cab. "I braked, but was going too fast and went straight through him. I pulled up and spent some time trying to find the man but there was no one in sight." When the report appeared in the local paper, several other motorists came forward to say that they had seen the same figure dressed in white. None of them had previously mentioned the incident, as they thought that no one would believe them.

In 1958 a cricket team from the Kenwood Manufacturing Company Ltd. had played a match at Milton Bryan and was returning to Surrey along the A5. They had reached a spot near the Packhorse Inn, between Dunstable and Markyate, when the driver of their mini-bus swerved to overtake a car. Unfortunately this resulted in a crash with an oncoming vehicle which left two of the team, Sidney Moulder and Jerry Rycham, both from Woking, dead. Three other people were badly injured in the crash. It seems that at least one of the victims may still haunt the area where he died.

Grid reference: TL049179

The Priory Ghost

In the Priory Church there occasionally appears the ghost of a canon or a former prior. The ghost first appears in the south-west corner of the church, as if he has just walked through the wall from where the Prior's house used to stand. Turning to the right, he walks along the south aisle of the church until just before the Lady Chapel. He then turns to the left and walks along the front of the church, stopping to genuflect in the direction where the original altar would have stood. Finally, he turns to the right and walks through the east wall of the church. Originally, the wall divided the public part of the church (the part that still exists) from the chancel which lay to the east, as the church was almost twice the length it is now. The ghost may be seen to pass through the wall but he has never been seen on the other side, in what is now the churchyard. The ghost is said to have done the walk eight times in a day, at each of the daily offices.

Grid reference: TL02122186

Sally the Witch

It is rumoured that burials were not permitted at the Priory Church for some time, partially over concerns about releasing an evil that is buried there. A long time ago a witch called Sally was burnt at the stake along with her cat and broomstick but she reputedly returned to haunt the priory which stood on the site where the Priory church now stands. Ghostly hands would box the monks around their ears and the altar candles were said to have burned with an evil green light. If Sally's ghostly fingers touched the prayer books the covers would be burnt. Numerous ways were tried to get rid of Sally, including exorcism, but none of them seemed to have any effect and the abuse of the monks continued.

Things eventually got so bad in the church that a palmer (a wandering mediaeval European pilgrim who carried a palm branch as a token of having undertaken the greatest of pilgrimages, to the Holy Land) was called in to remove the spirit. As the palmer began the service, Sally struck him so hard about the head that he fell to the floor of the Chancel. Eventually the palmer outwitted Sally by luring her into a bottle, though

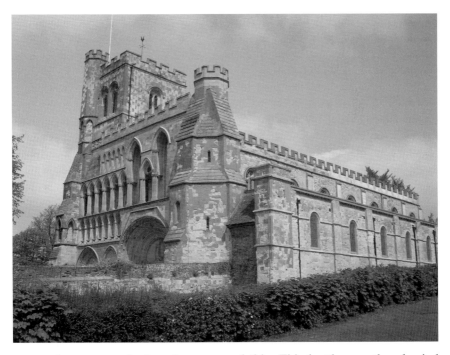

no one knows exactly how he managed this. This bottle was then buried somewhere in the grounds of the Priory church. Legend has it that for fear of breaking the bottle and releasing the witch no more burials were allowed.

Such was the tale when I first heard it, but since then I have found out a few more details which change the story slightly. The first detail which seems to be wrong, in the above tale, is that of the banning of burials in the churchyard so as to avoid breaking Sally's bottle. This is false, as the last public burials took place in 1861 and the last internment in a private plot was in 1933. It seems that burials were stopped as the cemetery was simply overcrowded. Today, there are only a few visible grave markers, which makes the churchyard look empty, but it is thought that there are over twenty thousand bodies buried there. The churchyard itself stands above the surrounding roads, with the extra height coming from the burials, one on top of another. There once stood a row of beech trees alongside the north wall of the church, some of which were blown down in 1809. The roots of the trees did not go deep into the ground, so when they were uprooted scores of bones came up with them. Eventually the cemetery was moved to its present site in West Street. It is true that Sally's bottle was buried in the churchyard and it even had a cairn of stones placed over it, but the stones have now gone, so the location of the bottle is unknown.

The church was originally much larger, so the land which lies to the east was originally inside the church. Next to the church, on the south side, stood a monastery occupied by Augustinian canons. The canons were not monks but priests, and as such they could have responsibilities outside the monastery, which included accommodating pilgrims who were visiting the church, one of whom was the palmer of the legend.

Sally was really just the village wise woman, skilled in medicines, midwifery etc., but she was not averse to casting the occasional curse for those who were willing to pay. It seems that Sally grew too big and powerful for the townspeople to cope with, so they complained about her to the prior. He did little, apart from providing them with talismans, for a suitable fee of course, to ward off anything Sally might do to them. But things steadily got worse; hayricks were burned down and children became ill, all of which was blamed on Sally, irrespective of the real cause. When the townspeople complained again, the prior was forced to act and Sally was tried and executed. The site of her execution was in the town square, where the clock tower now stands (grid reference: TL01992171). According to legend, as Sally was burned alive the Devil arrived on a bolt of lightning to take her away.

But, Sally did not go without a fight and her ghost returned almost straightaway, much to the dismay of the prior and canons who came in for some heavy abuse under Sally's invisible hands. Everything was tried to get rid of her, including exorcism, but to no avail. Now, it happened that a palmer was staying at the Hospital (the canons were Hospitallers, literally due to their providing hospitality) and both he and the prior tried to get rid of Sally. It is said that Sally came up to the palmer, but he stood his ground; instead of fleeing he produced a religious relic which caused Sally's ghost to back away in fear. The exact nature of the relic is unknown, but such items were usually a piece of the true cross or a bone from a saint, or similar artefact. The palmer walked towards Sally and she backed up until she reached the altar, where she stood transfixed. The palmer then raised his hands and said an incantation, whereupon Sally began to shrink until she was the size of his thumb. The palmer then calmly picked her up, dropped her in the bottle and sealed it. He then gave it to the prior and told him to have it buried in the ground. Such was the end of Sally's ghost. From here the legend of the bottle and the stopping of burials developed, because it was said that if the bottle was broken Sally would return with her powers increased ten fold.

Modern day townsfolk made use of the legend to scare their children into being good. An extra tale has it that the palmer left a small window in the bottle, which Sally could peer out of, and he even left her with some of her powers. Now, if Sally sees a child being naughty in the churchyard, she will place a spell on him/her.

Grid reference: TL02112187

Slaughterhouse

The area now occupied by The Freedom Salon in Ashton Square was once the site of a slaughterhouse, complete with ghost. It was believed that the ghost was that of a slaughterman, who was killed by a bull, which had decided to reverse the normal roles.

Grid reference: TL01902179

The Victoria

At the Victoria Public House, in West Street, there may be seen the ghost of a stable boy with an injured hand. The stable block stands at the back of the pub and it is this area that he haunts. It appears that he dates from Victorian times, and it is said that he trapped his hand in the stable door. No one knows why he haunts the area, but it may be that the injury prevented him from working, which in those days could have resulted in him starving to death. It is also possible that it was not the injury itself which killed him but complications, like an infection, which in those days could have been lethal.

Grid reference: TL01692176

The White Swan

At the White Swan public house, on High Street South, the bar is monitored by security cameras, which are linked to a screen in the living quarters upstairs. On the screen, there has regularly appeared the image of someone walking through the bar, but when you go downstairs there is no one there. Not only is there no one in the bar but, if you play the tape back, you will find that the figure was not recorded, yet he was clearly seen.

Grid reference: TL02162160

FLITWICK

Flitwick lies to the south of Ampthill and has a population of 12,160. The site has been permanently occupied since about 4000 BC, but did not rise to importance until the Romans built a road through the area linking Watling Street and Ermine Street. In Saxon times its name was *Fleotwic*, meaning a dwelling on the river.

The Mount is the remains of a mediaeval castle which has been preserved as a public open space. Flitwick Wood lies close to the town centre and is a three hectare expanse of mature oak and ash trees.

Flitwick Manor

Late in 1994 John Hinds, a purchasing director, had booked into Flitwick Manor for the night after a business conference in the area. Just after one in the morning he finally prepared for bed and turned off the lights in his room. Shortly after settling down to sleep he was disturbed by the feeling of something very heavy landing on the bottom of the bed. He sat up and turned on the light but when he looked there was nothing there. Puzzled he turned off the lights and settled down again to try to sleep.

About fifteen minutes later he was again disturbed but this time by a shuffling sound which seemed to be coming from the foot of the bed. Quickly he switched on the light and sat up. There, sitting at his feet was the silhouette of a woman looking towards the window. After an understandable hesitation he asked "Who are you? What do you want?" The woman did not respond and continued to stare at the window, before gradually fading away until there was nothing there.

After that Mr Hinds spent the rest of the night with the lights on, too afraid to go to sleep in the room. He was reported to have said "I detected that there was something in the room with me. I had a feeling there was a presence. I can't describe it."

Early the next morning he went to reception to check out. The receptionist, Lydia Dawson, asked if there was anything wrong as he seemed agitated. Mr Hinds told her that he had been visited during the night. Lydia said that he seemed slightly nervous and she didn't really know what to say to him. Basically she didn't really take any notice of it at the time.

Three days prior to Mr. Hinds encounter, Jim Sparkes, a builder who had been brought in to do some repairs and modifications, had removed some roof tiles at the front of the manor. Beneath the tiles was a wooden door which opened into a room that had not been used for a considerable time. Looking round the room he found an old doorway which had been bricked up and which had obviously led into the upper floor of the manor. It is strange how often ghosts appear when a building is being modified.

The manager of the hotel, Sonia Banks, often stayed over in the hotel after working late, and one night she locked up the building and retired to Room 8. She was the only person in the manor at that time. Not long after entering the room she heard the sounds of footsteps coming from the floor above. They appeared to go a short distance across the room above and then they just stopped. The sounds had come from the area where the small attic room had been discovered.

The manor's chef, Duncan Poyser, also had an encounter there that he will not forget. He had just gotten into bed in a second floor room and was drifting off to sleep at around ten minutes past one. When he tried to turn over, he found he couldn't move the bottom of his legs. It was as if someone or something was sitting on them. He tried twice more, and eventually managed to free himself, tumbling onto the floor. Duncan was reported to have said that it was just a really strange experience and a really strange feeling.

The night after John Hinds had his encounter with the spectral figure, receptionist Lydia Dawson was to have her own. She checked into Room 7 and went to sleep almost right away. She awoke suddenly and saw an elderly woman standing near to the bed. Lydia described the woman as wearing a long Victorian dress and a small white cap, but what struck Lydia the most was that the woman was crying, obviously in some distress. Lydia jumped up and fumbled for the lights, but after a few seconds she fled to the corridor outside. She had picked up on the emotions of the figure and was quite upset herself. Lydia said that she had never seen anything like it. After gathering herself up she bravely went back into the room, which was blazing with lights that she herself had not managed to turn on, due to her desire to flee the room, and found that the woman had gone.

Lydia was not the only one to see the elderly ghost, as she was also seen by the hotel's original owners when she walked across a room in front of an entire family who were at the hotel for Christmas. Other guests have also seen her and have even reported the smell of rose perfume when she is around.

The paranormal events soon quietened down and life at Flitwick Manor settled back into its routines once more, although no member of the hotel staff would stay overnight unnecessarily.

Flitwick Manor is a large Georgian building which is over three hundred years old. In 1798 it was taken over by George Brooks and remained as the family home for the next one hundred and fifty years.

One owner, John Thomas Brooks, kept a diary of life at Flitwick Manor and described the death of his daughter Mary Ann Brooks at the age of twenty-six on September 20th 1848 at seven o'clock in the evening. Her death was a great shock to the family and one from which Mary Ann's mother would never really recover. Though she outlived her husband by twenty years she died at the age of eighty-six, a senile and rather sad figure.

Is it possible that the tragic, elderly female figure seen by both John Hinds and Lydia Dawson was the late Mrs Brooks, mother of the ill-fated Mary Ann who died there one hundred and forty-six years before?

John Lyall, the last direct descendant of the Brooks family, spent his childhood in the manor and remembers his mother's references to the ghost. Many a time she heard it knocking on her bedroom door, and he recalls that the local villagers had always regarded the manor as being haunted. Not long after John Lyall left Flitwick Manor it was sublet to different residents, before it was finally converted into the current hotel.

Grid reference: TL02893417

The Swan

The Swan, in Dunstable Road, is said to be haunted by a ghost who has the irritating habit of hiding things. It seems that the miscreant is somewhat of a practical joker, as he will also move things around, much to the annoyance of the staff members. He seems to like to target people who are new to the public house. If you are a new member of staff, you may find your jacket and belongings are no longer where you left them.

Grid reference: TL03413490

GOLDINGTON

Goldington is a large residential area which lies to the east of Bedford town centre. There has been a settlement on the site for a considerable period of time, even pre-dating Goldington's entry in the Domesday Book (*Goldentone*).

Goldington Hall

There are two ghosts that are known to haunt what is now the Lincoln Arms, formerly known as Goldington Hall. One is an elderly lady in Victorian dress that haunts the window seat on the landing. She usually appears in the evening and there is a cold spot around the window seat although there is no source of a draught. The other ghost is heard but has never been seen. She is thought to be a little girl, as about every three days childlike footsteps are heard on the upper landing. The assistant manager has often heard the sounds of a child's footsteps, but every time he has run up there he has found nothing.

The landlady's Golden Retriever, Harvey, will not venture upstairs and has even been known to run away as if he was scared. A previous manager had a large Great Dane which knew no fear, but it refused to go into the Pistol Bar area. The present manager believes there are four tunnels that are connected to the local church and which were once used to carry dead bodies from the Hall so that they could be moved unseen by prying eyes. Three of these tunnels are supposed to run from the Pistol Bar area.

Goldington Hall dates from the time of Cromwell and there are some lead rainwater pipes bearing the date 1650. The first known occupant was Nicholas Luke, as noted in the records of the Hearth Tax of 1671. At that time the building had ten fireplaces and was taxed at £1 per year. The first officially recorded owner was Sir Thomas Allein who sold the hall in 1680. Little else is known about the ownership of the hall until 1843 when the owner was Robert Faulkner. At that time the hall was occupied by Lord Francis Russell, a relative of the Duke of Bedford.

William Kenworthy Browne moved into the hall in July 1844 and Edward Fitzgerald, the translator of 'The Rubaiyat of Omar Khayam', became a regular visitor. In 1859 William was crushed by his horse on his way back from the hunt; he survived for two months before finally succumbing to his injuries. Goldington Hall passed to the Polhill family, then on to William Marsh Harvey in 1874. By that time the hall was a dilapidated version of its original self. Harvey spent three years restoring the hall, which left it looking much as it does today. Just after 1940 the house became owned by Bedford Corporation and was converted to flats. Then finally in 1972 it was purchased by Bass Charrington and converted into a public house (and, even now, it may be reverting back to flats).

Grid reference: TL07495071

The Grange

Several publications have printed the story about 'the ghost of a mad gardener, who had attempted to kill a former owner of the hall, and was seen staggering around the grounds with a pitchfork through his heart'. This story was originally attributed to Goldington Hall, but in fact the events took place at the Grange which was demolished some considerable time ago.

Grid reference: TL072504

HARROLD

Harrold is best approached from the south, as you get a remarkable view of St. Peter's church amongst the trees in the background and the mediaeval bridge across the river in the foreground. The village lies to the north-west of Bedford and has a population of 1,170.

The bridge was first mentioned in 1278-9 and is located in the corner of four parishes. Because of this it was required that four separate lords of the manor maintain the bridge so that each was responsible for one arch. This led to a large variation in styles from one arch to the next. The High

Street is lined with stone-built houses and cottages in the middle of which is the village green. The green is unusual in that it contains a strange round lockup with a steep roof. The early eighteenth century Market House also stands on the green.

Harrold Road

About three years ago on a February morning a man was driving home from work after completing the nightshift. He had reached the Harrold Road, which runs from Lavendon to Harrold, at about a quarter to seven when he spotted a bird lying in the lane. In his headlights it looked like a hen pheasant which he only just managed to avoid running over. He drove on to a spot where he knew he could turn round so that he could go back and check on the bird. As he reversed into a farm entrance he saw another car coming up the lane and watched as it suddenly swerved, presumably to miss the bird, then it came to a stop.

As the nightshift worker approached the scene, he saw that the other driver had stopped on the wrong side of the road. The driver had gotten out of the car and was standing looking back at the bird six metres behind his car. The driver was a young man wearing jeans, a grey jumper and a red woolly hat. As the nightshift worker approached, the young man did not move, so he had to drive round him, then avoid the bird. The way the man was acting appeared to be very odd, so the nightshift worker carried on down the lane for twenty metres before doing a 'U' turn at a turning off the lane. As the driver swung round he was amazed to see that the bird, the young man and his car had all vanished. The driver had a clear view right up the lane but there was no sign of them; he was completely alone there in the grey light of dawn. What struck the driver as being odd was the fact that as he passed the young man he never moved a muscle or even looked at the car that passed close by him.

Grid reference: SP935549

High Street

Two Police Officers who were stationed at a rural Police station in the north of the county were patrolling the village of Harrold at between three and three thirty in the morning. It was a cold and very foggy weekday morning in 2002, even though it was supposed to be summer. Because of the fog they were driving slowly as they turned into the High Street from the Odell Road (grid reference: SP95545692). Driving towards the green in the middle of the village (grid reference: SP95105680) the fog suddenly lifted and they could see the stars for the first time that night. One of the officers made the comment about how spooky it was, like a night out of a scary movie, but neither could remember who had voiced their thoughts. Just then the officer who was the passenger pointed out a bike rider in front of them who looked out of place because of the bike she was riding.

The bike was an all black tricycle looking like it had come from Victorian days. Between the two back wheels was a wicker basket and the front headlight looked like an oil lamp. The rider was a Caucasian female in her early thirties, slim with long dark hair, to the middle of her back, hanging loose. She appeared to be wearing an all-in-one sleeveless black dress which seemed inappropriate for the weather. The bike appeared to be of the old style where the pedals are linked to the drive wheel, so that you had to constantly pedal and couldn't free wheel. She was constantly pedalling at the same slow speed without deviating from her course or changing how she sat. The passenger commented that she was a ghost but his colleague dismissed it, even though it was freezing and the officers were wrapped up well, whilst she was only wearing an inappropriate, sleeveless dress.

The passenger suggested that the driver pull over but he drove on past the rider; his colleague felt that he didn't stop as he was a bit scared. As the officers slowly drove past the passenger stared at the rider through the window, but not once did she glance to one side. They were feet away, but she never moved, she just kept up her constant pedalling.

As they passed, the passenger commented to the driver that she was definitely a ghost; they turned around to look at her but she was gone. In the twenty seconds it took to turn the car around she and the bike had completely vanished. At the time she was some way away from cover on a street with poor but adequate lighting. Since then the police officers have never encountered the rider again, even though they patrol the same area in Harrold at about the same time of night.

Recently, I have heard a different interpretation of the tale. This was related to someone I know, by two men in a public house in Harrold, late one evening in January 2005. In their version, the woman was a local who had been to a fancy dress party and was returning home. A few things do not make sense about this interpretation. Firstly, it was three in the morning on a weekday, odd time for a party! Second, the bike was a tricycle with no gears, which must be a rare thing today! Third, an oil lamp? Fourth, why did she ignore the patrol car? I like rational explanations but this one, related in the pub, seems to add more questions than it answers. The ghost version is a much simpler answer.

Grid reference: SP951568

The Oakley Arms

The Oakley Arms in Harrold appears to be haunted by the ghost of a former landlord, Dan Orpin. Dan ran the pub during the thirties and forties and since his death he has appeared in front of drinkers many times. He either runs through the pub or he has been seen sitting, smoking a cigarette and drinking a pint. His footsteps are sometimes heard upstairs, but his preference is to sit in the bar with the other customers, almost as if he never died.

Grid reference: SP94945689

HOUGHTON CONQUEST

The village name of Houghton Conquest is derived from the Old English words '*Hoh*' and '*Tun*' which means a farmstead on or near a ridge or spur of a hill. The Conquest aspect of the name is that of an important local family in the thirteenth century. The village contains the largest parish church in Bedfordshire.

The Knife and Cleaver

The Knife and Cleaver in Houghton Conquest is haunted by two ghosts, one thought to be male and the other female. A young student barman was rather shocked when he saw the pages of the booking diary turning over of their own accord. He was deeply shocked when a spectral hand suddenly appeared over his shoulder. It is said that virtually every day you will feel a draught as if someone has walked past you, but there is never anyone there to have caused the draught.

Grid reference: TL04404140

HOUGHTON REGIS

Houghton Regis is a mainly urban community which merges with the northern edge of Dunstable. The town has seen very extensive house building over the last fifty years, a lot of which were built to accommodate the London overspill. Houghton Regis now has a population of 15,840, though this may increase dramatically with the proposed addition of 25,000 houses in the area, many of which will lie to the north of Houghton (in the area around Thorn).

Despite this the old village green still survives, as does Houghton Hall, a fine chequer-brick mansion dating from about 1700. The grounds of the hall are now partially a public open space and partially new industrial development.

The parish church of All Saints is a very fine example of perpendicular architecture built from flint and the local limestone (Totternhoe Clunch) in a chequer-work style.

To the north-west of the town lies the small hamlet of Thorn. Here can still be found the Baptist cemetery from which John Bunyan preached to vast crowds.

other graves of a later date nearby containing beads, brooches, buckles and other objects.

To access the path from the Houghton Regis end go to the top of Millers Way (grid reference: TL01272373) and at the end of the road where it joins Coopers Way you will see the start of the footpath directly in front of you. Follow the path and keep going in a straight line until you reach the edge of the quarry; the path follows this edge. From Chalk Hill the footpath is signposted directly opposite the Chalk Hill public house across the A5. Follow the path down the steps and turn left down the small road; the footpath runs alongside a cottage on your right. The path runs through trees then emerges into a field below the quarry. Bear to your right up the hill until you reach the quarry edge.

Grid reference: TL006237

Sundon Road

Sundon Road in Houghton Regis is now fully developed with housing estates both sides of the road, but thirty years ago fields lay alongside part of the road with a thick boundary hedge. One night in spring Mr. Tony Broughall was returning to Luton after visiting his future wife, who lived in Recreation Road (grid reference: TL02372461), and was walking down the Sundon Road as he had missed the last bus. He was walking towards East End, Houghton Regis, where the Chequers pub stands (grid reference: TL02312417), when he saw a dark shape cross the road some distance in front of him. He could just make out what appeared to be the outline of a head and shoulders and assumed the figure was on a bicycle. As he rounded the bend before the well lit junction he could see that there was no one there (grid reference: TL02302450). The only way the figure could have disappeared would have been by pushing through the thick, unbroken hedge. Tony thought little of it and continued his journey home.

A week later he was repeating the journey when he was suddenly pushed violently from behind. So vicious was the attack that he almost fell into the ditch at the side of the road. The shock was amplified because he neither saw nor heard his assailant, either before or after the event, even though he searched the area.

One wet night some time later as he hurried along the same road he became aware of a strange, tuneless whistling coming from somewhere behind him. "The notes were aimless and jumbled and whoever or whatever was producing them seemed in no need to pause to draw breath." As he walked on, the sound got nearer and nearer. Eventually he could stand it no more and ran the last hundred metres to the well lit junction. "When I looked back, there was only the patter of the rain to be heard, and nothing to see."

From that time on Tony decided to make sure he caught the bus home. A few days later the conductor on the bus commented on how full it was that night. A teenager on the bus responded by saying that after what had happened to him he would be catching the bus in future. Tony was intrigued and went to sit beside the youth to find out what he meant by his comment. It transpired that he had been riding his motor scooter between Recreation Road and the junction at East End one night when a black shape, the height of a man, shot out of the hedgerow in front of him. He swerved violently, lost control and fell off his scooter. When he picked himself up he was surprised to find that the road was empty.

Grid reference: TL023245

KEMPSTON

Kempston lies to the south-east of Bedford town centre to which it is now effectively joined, though it is still a town in its own right. It is the site of the Bedfordshire Police headquarters. The present day population stands at 18,520. Within the town is the Saxon Centre which is a shopping precinct that has been built on the site of a Saxon cemetery.

Church Walk

Unusually a 'Green Lady' haunts a path in Kempston which starts at the end of Water Lane and runs past the River Great Ouse to All Saints

Church. In 1968 a newspaper article told of how the ghost would jump out at children from behind the trees that lined the path or sometimes she would be seen gliding in 'a sinister fashion' through the mist that was rising from the river.

It became so bad that bell-ringers and Cub Scouts stopped going to their evening meetings at the church for fear of meeting her. It is believed that she is the ghost of a woman who drowned in the nearby river many years previously.

Church Walk can be accessed from the A5134 (Kempston High Street). Follow the High Street west until you come to Water Lane, which lies on your right (grid reference: TL02314731). Follow Water Lane for about one hundred and fifty metres (mind the brook on your right as there is no fence) until it turns sharp left. Continue to follow the road for about one hundred metres until you reach a barrier across the road (grid reference: TL02094746). This is the point at which the footpath starts. It is just possible to park on the side of the road, as you come round the sharp bend; everywhere else the road is too narrow.

Grid reference: TL017475

Hillgrounds Road

In an area off Hillgrounds Road lie the ruins of Kempston Manor and a boathouse belonging to Kempston Youth Club/Outdoor Activity Centre. Whilst working at the site back in the 1980s Clem Tite, a storeman/technician, had several ghostly experiences. Clem said that almost every afternoon in the summer he used to hear footsteps in the building. He would search the place, but there was never anyone there. Clem was not the only one to hear the footsteps, as other people have heard them too.

Jackie Jennison, one of the youth workers, brought her German Shepherd dog, Evie, in one day. As she walked down a corridor to a room at the end, she suddenly became aware that the air was icy cold, as if she had walked into some huge refrigerator. The dog was also spooked so that it howled and its hair stood on end. Eventually it ran off with its tail

between its legs. One of the cleaners also had a dog and that also refused to go into the room.

About an area that once used to be meadows a story persists of a shepherd who was savaged to death by his faithful German Shepherd dog. Does his ghost return to keep dogs away from the area?

Grid reference: TL02774797

Kempston Manor

One evening the owners of nineteenth century Kempston Manor were returning home after attending a Christmas Eve Ball. As they approached the house their young son heard the sounds of the carriage and ran out to greet them. Unfortunately this resulted in his being trampled to death under the horses' hooves. Now on Christmas Eve can occasionally be heard the sounds of the carriage, the neighing of the horses and the screams of the boy.

The manor is now part of the Greys Education Centre, a Pupil Referral Unit that aims to support pupils who have been excluded from school, for any of a number of reasons.

Grid reference: TL02674770

Ladies' Walk

An area in Kempston known as Ladies' Walk is said to be haunted by numerous female spirits. Two are those of girls named Sophia and Frances who used to walk the area hand-in-hand and still do so after death. Other ghosts include Lady Snagge (see the entry under Cranfield: Wood End Lane) who is heard calling for her lost son, and another girl mourning the death of her Cavalier lover.

I am unsure as to the exact location of Ladies' Walk; all I know is that it was supposed to run alongside a Roman road.

Grid reference: TL025471

KENSWORTH

The village of Kensworth lies south of Dunstable in the north-east end of the Chilterns and has a population of about 1,500.

There has been a settlement on the site since Palaeolithic times (before 10,000 BC) and it is mentioned in the Domesday Book. The Romans also had a presence in Kensworth, but once they left most of the area reverted to scrub and woodland. The earliest reference is in 975 AD to *Caegnesworde,* meaning Caegin's farm. It is believed that the original farm boundary became the parish boundary of Kensworth.

Footpath Number 4

Three ghosts are alleged to haunt Footpath No. 4 in Kensworth. These consist of a headless milkmaid, a witch and Shuck (Anglo-Saxon scucca or sceocca: Satan), a one-eyed black retriever (for more details see Chapter 2: Black Shuck). The footpath runs between Common Road and

Hollicks Lane and is also known as the Coffin Route. The reason for its more gruesome name is because in the past people who could not afford a hearse to take a body to St. Mary's churchyard at Church End would carry the coffin along the path.

Church End (see entry) is also haunted by the ghosts of a milkmaid and a witch, both of whom haunt a path which runs north from the churchyard. The path to Kensworth lies to the south, on the opposite side of the church, so do both spirits haunt both paths, or has the location of the haunting become confused? No details are available about the Kensworth ghosts, but the Church End ones have good descriptions, so is Church End the real haunting?

The entrance to the path at the Kensworth end is located off Common Road. Follow the road from the A5 into the village until you pass the Post Office on your left. Fifty metres past the Post Office you will see a driveway on your right with the green footpath sign (grid reference: TL03251803). Follow this driveway in a straight line until you reach a field. From here you will see the footpath clearly marked and going diagonally across the field to you left. At the far end of the path you will reach a road (grid reference: TL03031887), follow this road down hill to your right to reach the church. Footpath Number 4 can also be accessed from a point three hundred and fifty metres further down Common Road at grid reference: TL02891815.

Grid reference: TL031185

KEYSOE

In the eleventh century Keysoe was known as *Caisot, Caissot* or *Chaisot*. Until 1870 it was one of the few villages to have a school which was maintained by the National Society for the Propagation of the Gospel.

Keysoe windmill, built in 1800, was the last working post mill in Bedfordshire and the only wind powered one that was still grinding flour in 1935. It was blown down in 1947.

College Farm

During the time of the enclosures, when public land was effectively being taken into private ownership, a man by the name of Matcham was once hung from an elm tree for stealing sheep. All that now remains is the stump of the tree, which can be seen in the corner of a field behind College Farm.

It is said that if you approach the tree at twilight and say 'Matcham, Matcham, I've brought you some broth', you will hear a disembodied voice reply 'Cool it!'

Grid reference: TL07036160

LEIGHTON BUZZARD

Leighton Buzzard lies on the west edge of the county and was originally two villages, Leighton and Linslade. The villages stood either side of the grand Union Canal and were united in 1965. The current population is 33,620.

In 1865 a row of six terraced Italianate style townhouses was built in Church Square by John Dollin Bassett. To encourage people to buy the houses they were offered for sale with a free season ticket to London on the nearby West Coast mainline railway. The tickets were for First Class travel and covered a period of twenty one years.

The Bedford Arms

If you want to get a good night sleep in Linslade, Leighton Buzzard, then room three of the Bedford Arms, in Old Road, is probably not the best choice. This room is said to be haunted by the ghost of a woman who has a habit of leaning over people when they are trying to sleep. The events usually occur between 2 and 3 am, and have ruined many a guest's sleep for that night. The woman has been described as wearing a long grey dress with a brown pinafore. People have also said that she has brown hair which is worn in a bun.

Drury Lane

Mr. and Mrs. Doerrer were walking past the Green in Houghton Regis late one night when they saw the figure of a young girl approaching. It was a cold night and after midnight, yet the young girl seemed totally unconcerned by both the lateness of the hour and the coldness of the weather, even though she was only wearing what looked like a flimsy white party dress. The young girl passed by the Doerrers without so much as a glance at them and it was then that they noticed that she was not only poorly dressed for the weather, but that she was also bare footed. Somewhat concerned they followed the girl into Drury Lane, but to their surprise there was no sign of her and all the houses were in darkness. They spent some time searching the area for the girl but to no avail before carrying on their way.

The Doerrers were later to discover that the figure of the girl had been seen by other people as far back as the 1930s. It is believed that she is the ghost of a little girl who was accidentally run over and killed by a car when returning home from Sunday school one afternoon.

Grid reference: TL02162396

Puddlehill

A footpath which runs from Puddlehill, just off Chalk Hill, to Houghton Regis has long been haunted by the ghost of a Saxon Chieftain. The area has a strange feel to it and occassionally the ghost would appear clad in full armour, though there have been no recent sightings.

The tale was given greater credence when, in the 1950s, a team of archaeologists from Manshead Archaeological Society unearthed the grave of an early Saxon warrior at the highest point of Puddlehill. The warrior had died a sudden and violent death as his skull had been smashed by a strong blow just above the left ear. Even though the grave was six feet long, the warrior had had to be bent to fit into it, with his head forced to one side and his spine twisted. The burial was a pagan one, with the warrior's shield and spear buried with him. Further investigation revealed

The name, The Bedford Arms, is just the latest name by which this hotel is known. In Pigot's Trade Directory of 1830, the pub is named the Corbet Arms and was owned by William Cotching. The name, Corbet, is that of one of the Lords of the Manor of Linslade, who took over the manor in 1688.

Grid reference: SP91482507

The Buckingham Arms

The ghost that haunts the Buckingham Arms is one who does not have regular habits. Unlike a lot of ghosts, months may pass before it again becomes active. When the ghost does return, it starts out by opening the front gate, early in the morning, walking up the path to the public house, then knocking loudly on the door. This is just the beginning.

From then on the life of the Buckingham Arms is filled with noise. This can range from the sound of heavy footsteps running up the stairs, to bangs and crashes coming from the cellar. The ghost will also go from room to room upstairs opening all the doors and slamming them shut. Or so it sounds, but no door has ever been seen to move. The same applies to the cellar, where it sounds as if the barrels are being smashed, but there is never any damage, only the sounds.

No one knows why this ghost is there, or why it chooses to act in such a violent way. Is there something which angered it? Now it vents its anger by making a lot of noise, but that is all it is, just noise.

Grid reference: SP91262515

Lake Street

It is strange how often alterations to a building can stimulate or even start a haunting. Sid Mularney certainly discovered this when he decided to do a bit of DIY to his place of work. On Tuesday 28th May 1963 the 'Beds and Bucks Observer' carried the story of the goings on at Sid's workshop in Leighton Buzzard two weeks earlier. Sid, a motorcycle expert and dealer, had decided he needed more room in his workshop so he removed a partition. Unfortunately, in so doing he unleashed a poltergeist which wreaked havoc on his life.

The morning after he had removed the partition Sid arrived at work to find that three racing motorcycles, belonging to a local rider, had been knocked over and the fairings smashed. At first he couldn't work out what had happened, but eventually he decided that one of the bikes must have fallen over and had taken the other two with it.

A few days later Sid stayed late at the workshop as he was working on a racing gearbox that required urgent work. It was three in the morning before he finished and he was just getting ready to leave when "I felt something rush by me. I looked around and spanners were flying off hooks on the wall and a tarpaulin that was covering a bike took off and soared into the air." The whole place had become a mass of flying nuts, bolts and cycle parts. Sid grabbed a hammer to defend himself against the frenzied attack, but who was he defending himself against, as all he could see was flying metalwork?

Other surprises were to come. One morning when he arrived at work he found that a large box which had been full of nuts and bolts was tipped out all over the floor. The box was so heavy that Sid himself couldn't have lifted it but something certainly had. Other instances included petrol tanks being moved around, and large bolts, which Sid couldn't have mislaid, kept disappearing. All of the above occurrences took place during the night when Sid was away from the workshop and it was securely locked.

The owner of a nearby restaurant said that she had been woken several times during the night by "strange banging and clattering" which had been coming from Sid's workshop, but she was never able to find out what was causing it.

After a few weeks things quietened down and returned to normal, as is often the case with these events.

A local lady recalled that a strange rambling house once stood on the site of Sid's workshop. It used to have a huge cellar but she would never go down there as it was 'so old and weird'. The cellar would have stretched underneath the workshop. The premises had once been a basket-making factory and tradition has it that a man hanged himself there. It is unlikely that the blame lay with the ghost of the dead man, as there had not been any ghostly activity prior to Sid's alteration work. The workshop has now gone due to rebuilding work and improvements to the local roads.

Grid reference: SP923249

LUTON

Luton lies to the north of a gap in the Chiltern Hills which has been formed by the River Lea. One of the town's earliest names is *Lygetun* which means 'the enclosure by the river Lea'. The current town covers an area of thirty square kilometres, but a hundred years ago the streets and houses covered somewhat less than three square kilometres.

For centuries Luton had just been a small farming community, then it became a market town but had started to fall into decay by the seventeenth and eighteenth centuries. In the early nineteenth century the development of the straw plait industry saw Luton's revival until it became the major centre for hat manufacture in the south-east Midlands. Later still, Luton became the centre for Vauxhall Motors and other manufacturing industries, but now most of them have gone.

Alma Cinema

The Alma Cinema used to stand on the corner of Alma Street and New Bedford Road in the centre of Luton. From the day it was built people thought that it was a strange place. People spoke of "an uneasy, oppressive atmosphere" which filled the rear of the building from the ground floor boiler room right up to the projection room at the top. This area of the building was used exclusively by members of staff and consisted of two concrete staircases feeding a virtual maze of rooms and passages. Some people claimed that as they went up the stairs they felt that something was moving up with them, always keeping one flight in front. Coming downstairs was worse, as people felt that they were being followed and whatever was doing the following was just waiting to push them down the stairs.

When the cinema was demolished, an old cap said to be heavily encrusted with blood was found in the circle girder work. Did this belong to a workman who is said to have fallen to his death from the roof girders? No one knows how he fell but some say he'd had one beer too many, whilst others maintained that he was knocked off balance by a colleague and plummeted to his death. Could it be the ghost of this unfortunate man whose presence was once felt in the building? As the original building has now gone we may never know.

The Alma cinema was built to accommodate over sixteen hundred filmgoers and had its opening night just before Christmas 1929. The Alma was very lavishly decorated and even had a restaurant above the cinema with an eighteen piece ladies orchestra. Even before it was built there were whispers that it would never be a success. The area had previously been occupied by terraced houses and cottages which had to be cleared away to make room for the cinema. The people who lived there were angry at being moved and some feel that they cursed the cinema. Towards the end of 1943 the Alma went over to variety shows, then alternately films and stage shows. Later it became the Cresta Ballroom before finally being demolished in 1960. The more modern Cresta House business premises now stands on the old Alma site.

Grid reference: TL08942142

Bridge Street

The Galaxy Centre in Luton is a complex containing a multi-screen cinema, bars, restaurants and the Namco Game Station. In Screen 6 at Cineworld people have seen moving shadows but they have never been able to find the cause (at least not a natural one). They have also heard

some strange sounds and felt patches of ice cold air in the heated theatre. It is believed that something now haunts the theatre but no one knows who or what it is, or was.

The building stands on what was, for a short while, the Bridge Street car park. Some time prior to this the site was occupied by the Luton branch of the Co-op, and earlier still it was the site of the Crown and Anchor brewery. Ghosts were rumoured to appear in this area in the past, too.

Grid reference: TL09042152

The Cork and Bull

The Cork and Bull pub in Cumberland Street Luton is said to be haunted by the white vision of a lady who is known to move things around. She has also been known to shake tables and even throw bar stools across the room.

It is believed that she is the ghost of an old woman called Ann who lived in the pub and was murdered there, and now it is said that her soul can never find rest.

The ghost appears not to be confined to the pub as she has been seen in the area around the pub and is known to move along Cumberland Street, being seen at a different location each time. People have even been known to sit and talk with her in the pub, without realising what she is, and she has even responded by touching them.

Grid reference: TL09492097

Crawley Road

In the 'Luton News' of 6th April 1994 there appeared a report of a poltergeist in the house of Eddie Herbert and Sam O'Reilly in Crawley Road. The article in the paper was read by Mrs. Eileen Lewis who lived in Essex Close at the other end of Luton. Mrs. Lewis contacted the paper to tell them of her own experiences in Crawley Road. When she contacted the newspaper she was seventy years old, but she still vividly remembered her experiences in an old haunted house she had played in as a child.

The house stood in Crawley Road and twelve year old Eileen took up a dare from her friends to climb to the top of the deserted house and look out of a window to prove she had done it. "I went into a room, and then all of a sudden stones were flying around me; I don't know where from, they just came out of everywhere. I was so scared I ran down the stairs while the stones were all around me, but I was not hit by them."

Grid reference: TL086217

The Four Horseshoes

In 1876 the original Four Horseshoes public house was burned to the ground and the body of the owner was found by the back door. When he died he was still clutching a cash box which contained the night's takings.

Members of staff at the present Horseshoes have heard the sounds of money being counted when they are in the cellar and at the same time the air feels cold, even on a warm day. Is this the ghost of the 1876 owner, William Clifford, who has come back for his money? You may not be able to take it with you, but it appears that William will have a go, if he can.

Grid reference: TL09542097

Galley Hill

A hill called Galley Hill on the outskirts of Luton was, in former times, the site of a gallows, where public executions would have taken place. The site was also used to bury the bodies of local witches who where hanged during the witch hunts of the sixteenth and seventeenth centuries. Often these witches were no more than village wise women. All it took was for them to be accused by villagers who had a grudge against them. However, a strange discovery was made on the site during excavations in the 1960s. A steer skull was found with a die placed on top of it with the six uppermost, evidence of possible ritual usage in the past.

Gallows sites were often considered to be haunted, sometimes by black dogs and other fearful guardians, Galley Hill being no exception (see Chapter 2: Black Shuck). Places avoided by the local population would have made the best sites for clandestine rituals.

There are two routes you can follow to reach Galley Hill, both of which involve a reasonable walk. If you follow the A6 from Luton, for about four and a half kilometres, you will see Warden Hill Road on your right. Follow this road to the end (just under half a kilometre) and turn left into the car park (grid reference: TL08602591). You will now be at the foot of Warden Hill. From here you walk north for five hundred metres, then turn right along the path which leads towards Warden Hill. As the path starts to rise steeply you will see the path to Galley Hill on your left (going around the base of Warden Hill). If you want to get a bit closer, before you walk, you can park at the top of Turnpike Drive. This is the road to the right at the last roundabout on the Luton section of the A6. Follow this road uphill, bearing to the left. Just over three hundred metres from the A6 there is a small cul-de-sac on the left, at the end of which is the path (grid reference: TL08402649). The path is the one mentioned earlier, which takes you up to Warden Hill. A very pleasant walk can be had by parking along the road from the A6 Streatley roundabout towards Lilley. One and a quarter kilometres along this road there is a footpath on the right (grid reference: TL08712850). Follow this path across the fields to reach Galley Hill.

Grid reference: TL092269

Hastings Street

A business premises in Hastings Street in Luton seems to be home to several spirits. In the building the public side of the reception area is separated from the business side by a locked door which contains a tall, narrow, glass panel. Alongside the door is the reception desk, which is accessed through a separate door from the secure side. One member of staff remembers seeing a woman standing in reception near to the secure door, so she walked round behind the desk, and in the few seconds it took her to walk round, the woman had gone. She saw the same figure again about two weeks later, and once she just sensed that there was someone there, but she couldn't see anybody. She described the figure as a blonde haired woman, aged between forty and forty-five. She didn't notice anything unusual about the woman, just that she was wearing a dress and hat. All the sightings and feelings had occurred during daylight. The staff member said that, when she saw the figure, the woman was facing the secure door and looking down.

The reception area has a second door, which leads out to a stairwell and finally to the street. Any person entering reception would have to come through this second door. The door itself cannot be opened or closed without making quite a bit of noise, but no sounds were heard from when the staff member saw the woman until she had walked round to reception, so where did she go? A colleague, working late at night, once heard the reception door close, but on investigating found that there was no one there.

Other people have experienced strange feelings in the building, especially on the back stairs. One corridor in the building has a bad reputation, with members of staff feeling as if they were being followed as they walked down the corridor.

Back in the 1950s a murder took place near to the building, and it is said that the body of the female victim was brought in and laid out in the cellar. Could this be the connection to what is happening there now?

Grid reference: TL088209

Site Report

I was fortunate to be able to investigate the building along with members of the Luton Paranormal Society (LPS) one evening in July 2004. We were joined by a member of staff, a spiritual medium and a woman who is very sensitive to the paranormal. We concentrated on three areas of the building where things had been seen or sensed. These were the reception area, basement and the corridor where you are followed.

Basement

The group of which I was a member started our investigation in the basement of the building and obtained some interesting results very quickly. The medium was wandering around the basement when he approached an area where an LPS member was standing. He noticed that she kept touching her jaw and looked somewhat distressed. He enquired from her as to what was wrong and discovered that she was having the same feelings that he was. This amounted to a distinct ache in his jaw, which he described as the feeling you get if you chew metal. The LPS member, my daughter, also reported a pain in her stomach as all her muscles had tensed, her eyes watered and she felt as if she was about to vomit. The area in which this occurred was just in front of the entrance to the cellar, in an area where a presence had been felt by another staff member.

The medium picked up on the name Taylor, near one side of the basement, and the sensitive member of the team reported that her hands hurt and it felt as if she was trying to strangle someone. She said that she felt the presence of a man who had strangled a woman, and who now felt remorse and was seeking his victim. When the medium and my daughter approached the area they both felt tingling sensations in their thumbs.

Corridor

This particular corridor is 'L' shaped and it is in the shorter, five metre, section that a presence had been felt. Whilst investigating the corridor, the sensitive member of the team said that she saw a figure pass the end of the long arm of the corridor (about twenty metres away) several times. The area was investigated but nothing could be found.

The corridor was fairly dark with just enough light filtering in to make things visible. We set up a video camera to monitor the short arm of the corridor, while we investigated it. We felt nothing untoward as we stood in the short corridor, but one interesting event did occur which was captured on video. A member of staff and I were down the corridor near the far end, next to a window which looks into an adjoining room, discussing what had occurred there. My daughter was positioned two metres away back up the corridor, on the other side of the window, with a member of LPS next to her across the narrow corridor. The staff member said that she had always felt uneasy when inside the room looking towards that particular window. As we talked I suddenly felt a distinct cold shiver with nothing, that I could discern, that would have triggered it. The staff member then noticed that my daughter had looked round, so she was facing back up the corridor, and the LPS member had started shining his torch back along the corridor towards the video camera.

The staff member went to talk to the LPS member, and I talked to my daughter, who told me that she had felt something brush past her legs. This was odd as the corridor appeared to be unventilated and no-one had opened any of the doors along the corridor. I asked her when this had happened and managed to narrow it down to almost the same instant that I felt the cold shiver. The LPS member said that he had suddenly felt cold, which was why he was checking the corridor with his torch. On the video you can see my daughter turn round briefly (when she had the feeling on her leg), followed almost immediately by the LPS member turning round and turning on his torch. Within seconds of this the staff member stopped talking to me and turned to the LPS member, it was just before we stopped talking that I felt the cold shiver. It seems very likely that all three events occurred at almost exactly the same time, almost as if something had briefly passed along the corridor.

Garage

At the back of the building there is a large garage accessed from the end of a long corridor, described in the previous section. In the garage my daughter sensed that there was an old man in one corner (to the left of the entrance doorway, which lies opposite to the garage doors), trying to get up. She felt that he was aged between fifty and sixty years. The sensitive member of the team said that she had sensed a man who was drunk and called Eric. She felt that he was looking for the home he lived in. She also said that she felt that he was over sixty years of age and that he was angry at being disturbed, not just by us, but by all the other people in the building. When she and the medium had first entered the garage they had felt a rush of warm, humid air, which reeked of alcohol. She also reported that the man had choked to death on his own vomit.

Whilst in the reception area the sensitive member of the team managed to contact Eric and learned that he was a disreputable character from Stepney, who had come back as he used to have a room in the area. He was angry because his room had gone. He also had a scar down his back and said that he had killed another man, but at a different location. Further communication revealed that he was fifty-two years of age, dishevelled and wearing brown tweed. On his right cheek he bore a scar, caused by a knuckle duster during a fight with, or over, a woman; she also discerned that he was a pimp.

Highbury Road

At Highbury Road in Luton has been seen what has been referred to as the 'Luton Gasworks Ghost'. In 1961 Jack Boutwood saw the ghost and described her as having jet black hair and standing over six feet tall. She appeared to be aged about forty and Jack said she was wearing a white robe which hung down to her feet.

It was two o'clock in the morning when Jack left the gasworks where he was working for a quick cigarette. As he stood outside smoking he saw the figure of the woman gliding along the road towards him and realised she was a ghost. As the figure passed him by, Jack quickly jumped on his motorcycle and followed so that he could get a better look at her. When he returned to the gasworks Jack told a colleague, Bert Fleckney, about what he had seen and Bert was just in time to get a quick glimpse of her before she disappeared into Highbury Road.

The grid reference is for Highbury Road as it now appears; a cul-de-sac with a drop at the end into Waldeck Road. The gasworks was located at grid reference: TL084216.

Grid reference: TL083220

Hockwell Ring

A flat in Green Court, Hockwell Ring, was haunted by a malevolent spirit. Things were so bad that the couple who lived there were forced to call in an exorcist. The occupant, Jennifer Davies, described the figure as being dressed in a monk's habit and with a horribly scarred and disfigured face. The ghost would cause pots and pans to fly across the room and for things to go missing. One time it even shook the baby's cot violently. Sounds were also heard like a hot frying pan bursting into flames.

Neighbours told the couple that a man had died in the flat from burns and that his body hadn't been discovered for five weeks. After the exorcism the haunting ceased.

Grid reference: TL04952398

The Horse Shoe

In the seventeenth century a man named Cain was murdered in a field near the Horse Shoe public house in Leagrave Road. His corpse was carried into the pub and the suspected murderer was brought in and made to touch the body. When he did, blood poured from the wound and flooded the floor; enough evidence, so people believed, to prove that he was the murderer. For many years after the event the blood stains would reappear on the floor and then disappear once more.

This tale had me a bit confused. I was told that the pub was recently a hotel, but there are no hotels on Leagrave Road, the nearest being the Pines Hotel in Marsh Road (what the Leagrave Road becomes as you go north). Unfortunately this building is said to be Victorian in origin. The only other pub I could find with horse shoe in the name was the Three Horseshoes, which was actually in Leagrave and, strangely enough, at the end of the road which starts out as the Leagrave Road. This pub was still there in the 1889 but has now gone. Then I recalled that there was a building which had stood at the end of Marsh road, where it joins the Bramingham Road. The building was next to the island, on the site which is now occupied by the McDonald's restaurant. I also recalled that the building was destroyed by fire some years ago. This, in fact, was the Three Horseshoes, and I believe this is the pub of the tale, in Marsh Road.

Grid reference: TL06192427

Leagrave Road

At one time one of the largest employers in Luton was SKF in Leagrave Road, a Swedish company that manufactured ball bearings. In the 1970s SKF was booming, and it had its own resident ghost. The ghost was once a cook, and would appear in white overalls and white boots. She was once seen in 1973 by Mrs. Dora Rouget, a canteen stock controller, who said that she was very taken aback, but not particularly frightened. Not long after this the canteen was closed and the haunting stopped.

SKF was founded as Skefko (Svenska Kullagerfabrik) in 1907 in Gothenburg, Sweden by Sven Wingqvist. A purpose-built production plant was constructed in Luton on a one hectare site in Leagrave Road and production started on 17th June 1911. By 1924 SKF was employing one thousand people. In 1942 expansion of the company saw the construction of a second factory on Sundon Park Road. By 1977 all production had moved to Sundon Park and the Leagrave site was sold, whereupon it was renamed as Brittania House and the Brittania Estate.

Grid reference: TL078226

Old Bedford Road

The premises of Clegg and Holden in Old Bedford Road were haunted by a ghost who was recognised as being Mr. Clegg, a former founder of the printing firm. Mr. Clegg retired in 1950 and came back after he died, a few years later, to haunt the old Victorian house where the firm had its premises. A new employee last saw him in 1975 and described him as a slim man, about fifty, with a sunken face and wearing a grey suit.

Many strange things happened there including a mirror which smashed of its own accord. One employee had decided to clean it and another said that 'Old Cleggie' wouldn't like it, words which appeared to come true. Once several employees witnessed a rum bottle fly through the air. Jumpers and coats used to be thrown off hooks right across the room and a circular saw, which was driven by a very stiff foot pedal, would suddenly start to turn of its own volition.

A common occurrence was that of items going missing and turning up later in a completely different place. One incident involved a key which was always kept on top of a clock but one day was found to be missing. The premises were searched but there was no sign of it anywhere. It turned up several months later inside the clock, everyone denying that they had put it there.

Things were still happening in 1989 when a director of the company said "the other day we had a steel rule that suddenly disappeared and was later found hidden".

Members of staff always had the feeling that they were being watched, almost as if the old boss was checking up on them. At night the mains electricity would be turned off, but it didn't stop the lights from coming on by themselves when the building was empty. The firm of Clegg and Holden has now gone and so it seems has 'Old Cleggie', as the present occupiers of the building have not been troubled by him. Maybe Mr. Clegg's ghost really was looking after his own, earthly, interests.

Grid reference: TL090230

Wardown Park

The ghost of a former housekeeper once haunted the museum in Wardown Park. In 1971 two heating engineers were working in the cellar late one night when they heard the sounds of footsteps coming down the stairs behind them. They turned and saw a woman wearing a long dark

dress and carrying a large bunch of keys on her belt. The figure said
nothing, she just turned around and went back up the stairs. The two

workmen found the caretaker having a cup of tea and asked him about the
woman, but he said that neither he nor anyone else had been near the
cellar. After this the figure was never seen again but the sounds of
footsteps were heard on the stairs late at night or early in the morning.
Nothing has been seen or heard now for over twenty-five years.

The building was originally a Victorian Gentleman's residence
which came into the possession of Luton council early in the twentieth
century. It was used as a military hospital during the First World War and
it was at that time that the stories of the ghostly female figure started. The
figure, believed to be that of a housekeeper, would give both nurses and
convalescent soldiers a fright. A romantic story persisted that the ghost
was the spirit of a Victorian housemaid who had drowned herself in the
lake after an unsuccessful romance. Unfortunately this tale does not really

run true as the lake wasn't built until after the Council took over the building at the start of the twentieth century, well after the time when the housemaid was alleged to have drowned herself.

Grid reference: TL08932294

MARSTON MORETAINE

Marston Moretaine is a village to the east of Ampthill and has long been associated with the brick-making industry. The population is 3,870 and the village lies at the heart of an area called the Marston Vale.

Brick-making still continues in the area but many of the vast number of kiln chimneys have now been demolished.

Hillson Close

A house in Hillson Close had been plagued by paranormal phenomena for fifteen years before the occupier decided to have it exorcised. The haunting began with things disappearing but later the occupier, Janice Green, would find that she was waking up at night and being drawn to the window to look at the bottom of the garden. The vicar who turned up to perform the exorcism, the Reverend John Greenway, Rector of the Anglican Church in Marston Moretaine, believed that there was an evil spirit in Janice's garden. Janice had also been troubled by poltergeists which were possibly connected with the previous occupants of the house. After the exorcism the strange happenings ceased. Janice later discovered that the house was on the site of an ancient pond which may have been used as a ducking or swimming pond by witch finders.

Grid reference: SP995415

St. Mary the Virgin

The church of St. Mary The Virgin was built in the fourteenth century and is very unusual as the large church tower stands some way away from the main part of the church. It is believed that the tower was probably used as a refuge in Saxon times, either from flood or from attack. There are two Devil legends associated with the church and its tower. The first says that the tower used to be attached to the church but the Devil tried to steal it. The weight of the tower proved too much for him so he was forced to drop it in its present position.

The second legend says that the Devil had climbed up the tower and when he was challenged he leapt from the top of it. He landed one hundred feet away in a field where there is a prehistoric stone called the Devil's Jump. From there he took a second great leap and landed by a nearby public house, long since demolished, called the Jumps Inn, which was located on Station Road (to Lidlington), just south of the path which runs through the churchyard (grid reference: SP998408). He then took a third leap across the road and landed next to a group of boys who were playing leapfrog. It is said that the Devil joined them in their game, then he managed to trick them into jumping down a hole which led straight to his realm. In a slightly different version of the story the farmer who owned the field in which stood the Devil's Jump stone had played truant from church on the Sabbath to play leap-frog. It is said that the Devil then leapt off the church, landing on top of him and then, with a second jump, carried him off to hell. Now a dark figure is sometimes seen moving between the church and the tower but it has never been identified.

Within the church is the tomb of Lord and Lady Snagge; the latter is said to haunt the Wood End Lane in Cranfield.

Grid reference: SP99604117

MAULDEN

Maulden lies on the Greensand Ridge just under two kilometres east of Ampthill. The name means a hill marked with a cross. At the time of the Domesday Book the village was called *Meldone*. The area has been settled for some time, with Roman remains being found just south of the village. The village is bordered by Maulden Wood, one of the few remnants of ancient woodland left in the country.

Middle-Aged Ghost

If you are out and about in the village at night keep your eyes open, as the ghost of a middle aged gentleman is reported to follow people along the village footpaths.

Grid reference: TL052380

New Road

Ghostly monks complete with habits have been seen crossing New Road in Maulden but no further details are available.

Grid reference: TL058367

Silsoe Road

On the Silsoe Road the sound of a pony dragging chains can be heard, but nothing is seen. It is said that you can hear it going up and down Streets Hill.

Grid reference: TL060373

Tudor Ghost

In the village a boy wearing a Tudor ruff has been seen. It is said that he has a habit of playing pranks on the owners of the house he haunts.

Grid reference: TL052380

MILLBROOK

Millbrook lies very close to Ampthill and just to the west. It is said to be one of the most attractive villages in the country. It presently has a population of just 130. Originally the village was owned by the Duke of Bedford and many of the houses are one hundred year old estate cottages once occupied by the farm workers.

The church of St. Michael and All Angels lies on a ridge high above the village with a commanding view of the surrounding area. A wooded valley close to the church is said to be John Bunyan's 'Valley of the Shadow of Death' in 'The Pilgrim's Progress'.

Millbrook could also make the claim of being the most haunted village in Bedfordshire, as you will see from the sections below.

Galleytrot

A tale exists in Millbrook of a woman who, in the nineteenth century, became the victim of a supernatural black dog, locally called a Galleytrot. It is said that to meet one of these hounds means a death in the family and, sure enough, the poor girl was dead within three days. The hounds are a fearsome sight with red glowing eyes and as big as a calf.

The name is thought to be a corruption of 'gardez le tresor' (guard the treasure) though galley may relate to gallows (as in Luton's Galley

Hill where a gallows stood). It is said that large black spectral dogs are supposed to haunt such sites. Legend does have it that a Galleytrot is most likely to be found near a grave or a buried treasure. This would then connect with another legend about Millbrook, that of a buried pot of gold in Moneypot Hill. Black dogs are associated with the huntress Diana whose cult was prevalent in country areas. Other names for such beasts include Black Shuck and Padfoot. For a more detailed article on these dogs see Chapter 2.

Grid reference: TL013384

Sandhill Close

In the village the sound of horses' hooves can be heard racing down Sandhill Close but nothing has ever been seen. It is thought that the ghost is that of Galloping Dick, a highwayman who preyed on stagecoaches travelling along the busy Woburn Road to the south of the village. Dick lived in a tumbledown dwelling by the sandpit on Millbrook Hill (grid reference: TL01483809). He was eventually caught and hanged.

Parking is difficult along Sandhill Close, but the sand pit can be accessed from the A507. There are a couple of places to park just to the west of the road to Millbrook, at grid reference: TL01313805. The pit lies to the north of the A507, about fifty metres to the east of where you park. A hundred metres further east can be seen the Sandhill Close junction and the hill down which Galloping Dick races.

Grid reference: TL014381

St. Michael and All Angels

For quite a while the church in Millbrook rang to the strange sounds of cracking noises (said to sound like whips) and groans. A spectral glow was also seen emanating from the church when it should have been empty. Most of these events were attributed to the Huetts who had lived in a grand Tudor home in Millbrook, and whose tomb was in Millbrook Church.

In 1857 it became necessary to do some restoration work on the church, and the effigies of William and Mary Huett had to be removed. Their tomb was dismantled but for financial reasons it was never rebuilt. The two effigies remained inside the church but villagers came to believe that the Huetts were angry about being disturbed which was why the noises started.

In an attempt to quieten the suspicions of the villagers the rector had the effigies moved to the rectory cellar, but this had little affect as the noises continued. The rector's maid became so scared she refused to go down to the cellar and barricaded herself in her bedroom at night. Eventually the rector buried the effigies in consecrated ground in the churchyard but still the noises continued. Then in 1888 the chancel roof collapsed and an investigation revealed that it was riddled with death watch beetle. Many thought this was the explanation for the noises but some were not so sure.

In 1919 the rector, the Reverend H. P. Pollard, decided it was time to restore the Huetts to their rightful place, and a dig was undertaken by members of the Bedford Archaeology Society but they failed to find the statues. Mrs. Bunker, whose husband had been sexton, was known to possess a stone head that was found in the churchyard and eventually she revealed the general area where it was found. Sure enough the next dig found the statues and, after a little persuasion, the head was restored to its rightful place. The statues are somewhat battered, with that of William being minus an eye and an arm and cut off at thigh level. Mary has lost her feet and hands and most of her facial features but at least they are back in the church.

The church site is beautifully quiet and serene but a few years ago the then churchwarden, Mr. Jackson, had a strange experience. One night he was leaving the vestry and had just turned off the light when he noticed a hooded figure in black near the altar. He stood frozen in fear until the monk-like figure disappeared. It is thought that centuries ago a cell of St. Albans Abbey was set up in Millbrook and traces of monastic buildings have been found.

The church stands high on a hill and is accessed either from a footpath which starts in the village or a dirt road on the hill. The footpath lies on the right of the road as you come down from the A507 for about five hundred metres. The path lies directly opposite the Old Rectory, which is the first building you see on your left (grid reference: TL01293854). The path rises steeply up to the church entrance. If you travel by car you can park on the side of the road just before the Chequers restaurant and walk back (about two hundred metres). This is literally the only place you can park in the village. An alternative route is from the A507 just before you reach Sandhill Close when coming from Ampthill. On the right is an entrance to Warren Farm (grid reference: TL01613810) about seventy metres before the crossroads (signposted to the church). Go past the buildings on your left and just before a gate you will see a lane on your right with high hedgerows. Follow this lane to a crossroads (about one hundred and fifty metres) and turn left. Follow the new lane for three hundred metres to the church. These roads are really just dirt tracks complete with potholes, so be careful.

Grid reference: TL01363852

Station Road

The winding road that runs between Millbrook and the railway station is haunted by a headless horseman. It is possible that both this ghost and another who is heard in the village are Galloping Dick, a local highwayman whose victims were people travelling in coaches along the Woburn road to the south.

Grid reference: TL011389

Woburn Road

Long ago people returning from the Millbrook feast would walk along the path from the public house (which no longer exists) on Woburn Road past All Saints Church to the centre of the village. The point at which the path met the Woburn Road (the A507) had many strange tales associated with it. One tale involved a mother and her child who, one night, passed a pile of stones and saw them rise up into the air and fly around. Another woman saw a large black shape jump over a ten foot high hedgerow and land in the road without making a sound. Could this have been yet another instance of a sighting of Black Shuck, the proverbial Hell Hound? See Chapter 2: Black Shuck.

Yet another event was reported by a man who said that he had been followed by a strange light. The light had appeared by the aforementioned hedgerow and then it had followed him for a while before disappearing. By far the strangest tale must be of a man who climbed a stile near the same spot then suddenly found himself in Clophill, a distance of some ten kilometres as the crow flies. Unfortunately for the man the instant journey seems to have been one way only.

The entrance to the original path was at the point at which Ossory Farm now lies on the right of the A507 just before Millbrook, when coming from Ampthill. This entrance to the path has now gone, as it has been diverted via a rather tortuous and long winded route. Now it meets the Woburn Road on the right before Ossory Farm and just after the bend when travelling from Ampthill (grid reference: TL02023823). The path can be easily accessed from the A507 just before you reach Sandhill Close. On the right is an entrance to Warren Farm, about seventy metres before the crossroads, which is signposted to the church (grid reference: TL01613810). Go past the buildings on your left and, just before a gate, you will see a lane on your right with high hedgerows. Follow this lane to a crossroads (about one hundred and fifty metres), turn left to reach the church and right to follow the path back towards Ossory Farm. The path from Woburn Road to the church was virtually a straight line, but as you walk back towards Ossory Farm it now takes a turn to the left, away from the Woburn Road. If you project the straight part of the path forward until it reaches the Woburn Road, then you would have found the area where the above events took place. The grid reference below corresponds to this point.

Grid reference: TL01813819

Site Report

My first trip to Millbrook turned into a bit of a ghost tour visiting all of the haunted locations and places of paranormal interest in the village. This tour was part of a regular monthly trip with the Luton Paranormal Society.

It was late at night when we reached Millbrook by car, coming from the north-west along the road that runs from Manor Farm (just below How End north of Ampthill on the B530). We used this route as we had just visited Houghton House (just off the B530) and we wanted to enter Millbrook at the junction with the road to Millbrook station at the north end of the village (the road on which the headless horseman has been seen and heard).

We parked at the local hostelry (The Chequers) and set out south along Sandhill Close until we reached the path up to the church opposite to the old rectory. The rectory appears in the section on St. Michael and All Angels. We walked up the path from the road (grid reference: TL01293854) to the church, then spent a little while walking around the church grounds. The night was dry but there had been rain earlier on, so we were wary of taking pictures of moisture orbs and many photographs did show these. Nonetheless I did take one interesting picture at the church which can be seen at the end of the chapter on orbs (Chapter 4). In this image a large orb appears over the heads of the LPS members but it doesn't appear to be a moisture or dust orb. What is most unusual is the colour, a hint of yellow, which is unlike the artificially generated orbs I have photographed. These are usually blue/white, the colour of the flash on the camera, and a lot fainter. The colour could not have come from local lights as there aren't any and all torches were off at the time. This orb should be compared to the other ones in Chapter 4 which are considerably different.

After the church we followed the path towards the Woburn Road, then walked down Sandhill Close past where the old sandpit used to be (where Galloping Dick is said to have lived). The road down which we walked has the sounds of a ghostly horse, as described in the section on Sandhill Close.

MILTON BRYAN

Milton Bryan was the home of Sir Joseph Paxton who was a horticulturist and architect, and who was responsible for the design of the Crystal Palace for the Great Exhibition of 1851. St. Peter's church has a stained glass window which was donated by John's widow to the memory of her late husband.

To the north of the village stands a building which was purpose built during the Second World War as a radio station to transmit false information and propaganda to the Nazis.

On the 1889 to 1891 map of the area the village is referred to as *Milton Bryant*.

Mags Lane

Two men were walking back from the Eversholt feast on a rainy night when they saw a ghostly figure glide past them. To their horror the figure stopped, then it turned round and came back towards them. As they stood terrified, the figure peeped under the umbrella they were carrying. The men dropped the umbrella and fled to the nearest cottage. Later witnesses said that their hair "stood bolt upright with fear".

The ghost was that of Headless Mag who appears around midnight when a white, wraithlike figure manifests in a mist that comes up from a dell in the manor grounds, not far from Mags Lane. She then slips silently through the shrubbery to the lane that was named after her. People are unsure of when Mag lived in the dell but some believe it may be as recently as the beginning of the twentieth century.

When I first heard of this story the information said that the events happened 'near' Hockliffe at Mag Lane by the Manor House. Well, there was a manor house in Hockliffe but I could find no reference to Mag Lane. In addition the two men in the story would have had to have come down the Woburn Road into the centre of Hockliffe and across the Roman Watling Street and turn north to get to the manor. Then there are no roads nearby, only the road to Leighton Buzzard which is further south, so where was Mag Lane? So it must actually be Mags Lane in Milton Bryan nearly four kilometres away. If the men were walking back to Hockliffe from Eversholt, then Mags Lane would have been on the route they would have taken.

Moral: check all information first to see if it is valid. This is not the first time I have found inconsistencies in stories and it certainly won't be the last (this one of a site changing villages is very common).

Mags Lane comes off the A4012 at grid reference: SP96943001. From there it continues for three hundred and fifty metres into the village (grid reference: SP97233026). The Manor lies beyond the lodge, which is itself in line with Mags Lane. If you turn right at the end of the road and travel fifty metres towards the village centre you will see the Manor on your left.

Grid reference: SP972302

Site Report

My most recent night visit to Milton Bryan was at the end of February 2005, when I was accompanied by my daughter. We walked around the area of Mags Lane and the junction nearest to the manor, but there was nothing to report. Photographs taken in the area did display a strange set of misty shapes, tinted red, until further investigation revealed that these were caused by moisture condensing on the camera lens.

We decided to explore more of the village and set off past the Red Lion then turned right along the road which passes Fountaine's Farm, on the way to Town Farm. We walked past the village pond on our left, and continued to follow the lane until we reached a field entrance on our right. At this point, my daughter glanced sideways into the field and briefly saw a man wearing a dark coat and blue trousers about twenty metres away in the field. When she looked again he had gone, and we were unable to find anyone even though we searched the area. Where the figure was standing was in the middle of the field, with any hiding places at least seventy metres away, yet there was no sign of anyone. Oddly enough, photographs taken facing into the field, revealed the only orbs we saw that night. Were they mist or something else, and why did they only appear there and nowhere else?

MILTON ERNEST

Milton Ernest lies on the main A6 to the north of Bedford. It is a pleasant village on the banks of the River Ouse with a population of 680.

Milton Ernest Hall was originally designed by William Butterfield as a stone-built Victorian country house. It is now a private nursing home but in 1943 it was taken over by the US 8th Air Force Command.

In the last days of his life the band Leader, Glenn Miller, spent much of his time at Milton Ernest Hall before taking off from nearby Twinwood Farm Airfield in December 1944. The plane disappeared on the way to France and has never been found.

All Saints

On a hot summer's day Bill Turner, Bedfordshire's first real paranormal investigator, decided to go into All Saints church at Milton Ernest to get out of the heat. He had also decided that it would be a good time to see the church's beautiful stained-glass windows. He was in the church alone, sitting in one of the back pews, when the church doors opened. He heard footsteps walking down the aisle but there was no one there.

Bill decided to leave the church and turned round for one last look at the windows when he noticed a man in old-fashioned clothes and a silk top hat sitting in a front pew.

As Bill walked through the churchyard he spotted the sexton and went over to ask him about the man in the top hat. The sexton told him that there had once been a vicar in the parish whose wife died suddenly. Now, on the anniversary of her death, his ghost returns to the church. "And that", said the sexton, "would be today!"

Grid reference: TL02015611

NORTHILL

Northill has all the traditional village ingredients of a pond, public house and parish church. Nearby stands The Grange and the former Rectory.

The church of St. Mary was built in the fourteenth century and contains some fine mediaeval stalls and exceptional seventeenth century stained glass windows. The church also contains an unusual one-handed clock which was built by Thomas Tompion, the father of English clock makers, who was born in nearby Ickwell.

The Crown

Several customers at the Crown public house have seen the figure of a monk appear on the Green beside the pond. The spectral figure has then drifted across the pub car park before disappearing into Home Wood to the west of the pub. When Tony Dawson was the landlord at the Crown, his sons had a ghostly visitor. Tony was reported to have said that some years ago (around 1994) his sons encountered a figure in black coming towards them in the upstairs corridor one night. They both rushed back to their bedrooms to arm themselves with snooker cues but when they came out the figure had gone. The successor to Tony Dawson, Ian Taylor, said that certain areas of the pub have 'a presence' about them. There is an area behind the bar that is always warm as though someone else had just been standing there when there has been no one else about, and there is nothing to heat that particular spot.

The pub first appears in 1780 when the local vicarage was converted

to an inn. The cellars of the pub are supposed to be the entrance to a series of underground tunnels that connect the pub, the church and Ickwell Bury, formerly a monastery. The monks were from The Order of the Knights Hospitallers.

Grid reference: TL14914650

ODELL

Odell is one of the smallest of the Ouse Valley villages with only about 200 residences. It is situated to the north of the county and lies very close to the Buckinghamshire and Northamptonshire boundaries. It has a long association with the lace making industry but has more recently turned towards the leather industry. Odell has always been a farming community, with much of the land owned by Lord Luke of Pavenham and Odell.

All Saints Church was built in the fifteenth century on the site of a previous church. It contains a memorial to Lt. Richmond who was one of the crew members who died in the R101 disaster (see the section on Cardington: Airship Hangers).

Odell Castle

Sir Rowland Alston was a depraved and wicked man in life, and even in death he terrorised the village of Odell. It was said that he would walk through walls and tree trunks even in broad daylight. He rode a ghostly black horse and would ride into the hall of his family home leaving hoof prints in the flagstones. To get rid of him an exorcism was performed by twelve clergymen, all armed with bell, book and candle. His spirit was consigned to the village pond and remained there for one hundred years. Villagers who passed the pond said they could hear him snoring.

When eventually he emerged from the pond the devil was waiting for him. It is alleged that Sir Rowland had sold his soul to the devil but he was no longer willing to give it up. Sir Rowland fled to the church and squeezed through the keyhole. The devil shook the church in his rage and left five giant black finger marks on the jamb of the porch (unfortunately these were later removed by an over-zealous builder).

Now Sir Rowland appears every one hundred years driving a chariot and pair around his former estate. The next appearance is scheduled for 2044. Another version of the tale says that Sir Rowland appears at the church every one hundred years riding his black steed.

The Alston family had lived at Odell for three hundred years in a house on the site of the ancient Odell Castle. They were men of note, Justices of the Peace, Members of Parliament and soldiers.

Mrs. Ashton was once a servant in the house and had a frightening experience one day when she witnessed what she described as a smoky black insubstantial apparition. She was not the only one to see the ghost whose origin remains a mystery.

Grid reference: SP96815798

OLD WARDEN

Old Warden lies just off the busy A1, yet is one of the most picturesque villages in Bedfordshire. It is a small village with a population of 170 and a single street, yet this street is lined with thatched and tiled cottages set amid hedged gardens and with a backdrop of trees.

The general appearance and structure of the village was due to Lord Ongley, whose family had bought the estate in 1700. Early in the nineteenth century he 'prettified' it, then other, complementary houses were added by the Shuttleworth family who acquired the estate in 1872. The Shuttleworths and Lord Ongley were also responsible for the laying out of the Swiss Garden which lies just over a kilometre away to the north-east of the village and is open to the public.

The twelfth century St. Leonard's church contains a remarkable collection of carved woodwork brought from the continent in the early Victorian period. Some of the woodcarvings are said to have come from the private chapel of Anne of Cleaves, one of Henry VIII's wives. The church also contains some fine stained glass believed to have come from Warden Abbey.

The Hare and Hounds

In 2002 the barmaid at the Hare and Hounds, Michelle, was tidying up after all the customers had left. She looked up to see a woman standing by the bar. She glanced away briefly and when she looked back the woman had gone. Two years prior to this, renovations were being undertaken at the Hare and Hounds and a Spanish barman was staying overnight. It was a stormy night and he was alone when he saw the ghost of a woman in an upstairs room. A room at the far end of the pub called 'The Chapel' seems to be the most affected area.

Grid reference: TL13804395

Swiss Garden

Gardeners, who were working in the Swiss Garden, began to hear voices and sense presences that they could not see. It seems that during the restoration of the garden they had moved a stone cross which they had found and the thought was that this may have been the cause. They quickly returned it to its former location and the whispering stopped.

The garden was originally laid out in the 1820s to 1830s by Lord Ongley and it took its name from a summerhouse called the 'Swiss Cottage' that he had built there. The tale has it that his lordship had a Swiss mistress who bore him a son who unfortunately died at the age of nine. His grave in the garden was marked by a cross which bore no inscription. This was the cross that the gardeners moved. An alternative version of the tale says that Lord Ongley's Swiss fiancée was caught in a heavy shower of rain whilst she was walking in the garden. She sheltered under a tree but caught cold and later died, so that the grave is hers. Whichever story turns out to be true, the Swiss Cottage was built to the memory of Lord Ongley's fiancée.

Grid reference: TL148446

119

PAVENHAM

Pavenham is a lovely stone-built village on the banks of the River Ouse. It has a population of 670. The parish church of St. Peter is filled with elaborately carved Jacobean woodwork. This was only installed in the nineteenth century by Thomas Abbot Green when he came to live at The Bury, a large house which stood where the Bury estate now stands. During the Saxon period the village was named *Paba's Ham,* which became *Pabenham* in the Domesday Book.

According to local legend in 1665 a family called Hipwell brought mat making using rushes to the village and it became an important local industry. The Hipwells used to supply the matting for the House of Commons. The craft of mat making is still practised by the villagers to this day.

Church Lane

Church Lane is supposed to be haunted by the ghost of a Cavalier. The man had been stopped whilst leaving the village by a group of Roundheads and he had tried to escape by jumping his horse over a gate at the top of the lane. Unfortunately his horse clipped the gate and threw him. He was captured, executed and his body thrown into a nearby well. It is said that no gate, whenever built in the aforementioned gateway, can remain intact for long.

Grid reference: SP991560

High Street

A lady cyclist was riding from Pavenham towards Stevington and had just started to accelerate on a downhill stretch when she suddenly saw a large white dog in front of her. She was travelling so fast that she could not avoid hitting it. Imagine her surprise when instead of an accident she rode straight through the dog.

Grid reference: SP985554

120

PULLOXHILL

Pulloxhill is an old village being mentioned in the Domesday Book as *Polochessele*. In the eighteenth century it was the site of a gold mine. Part of the south facing slope of the chalk hill, on which Pulloxhill stands, has been purchased by the Parish Council as it has geological interest, being the site of a landslip, and it is also a rare ancient grassland site.

The Cross Keys

In the Cross Keys public house customers have reported seeing a grey lady and a man wearing a 1930s brown suit. The man was recognised by some people as being a previous landlord who had died in the pub.

In 1999 the pub was investigated by members of The Phantom Realm Society who saw shadowy figures strolling across the bar. They

also saw a very strange blue light, which appeared to move across the floor and seemed to glow of its own accord.

The landlord, Peter Meads, and his wife Sheila had been at the pub for thirty years. They said that the female ghost likes to sit in the inglenook fireplace, which is very unnerving for the customers. Without even seeing the ghost some customers will not sit in the fireplace as the atmosphere is said to raise the hairs on the backs of their necks.

One customer had a cast iron lion fall off the fireplace onto the plate from which he was eating a meal. The incident was inexplicable as the lion was fixed in place.

Grid reference: TL06313407

RAVENSDEN

There does not appear to be any reference to Ravensden in the Domesday Book of 1086 even though the site was certainly occupied at that time. Later the whole parish was owned by the barony of Bedford, so it is likely that in 1086 Ravensden was included in the fief of Hugh de Beauchamp.

Newnham Priory was founded in the parish of Ravensden in 1247 and was occupied by Augustinian canons from Bedford. After the Dissolution in the early 1500s the estate of Newnham Priory was called Ravensden Manor. It seems to have been built on land bestowed by Nicolas de Ravensden who was clerk to the then prior. Initially the land was seized by Henry VIII, and later it was granted to John Gostwick in 1540.

The Old White Lion

When Ray Close and Helen Britton purchased the Old White Lion it took a while between the purchase of the property and their actually taking up residence. Before moving in, Helen picked a single pink rose from the garden, which was the only one in bloom at the time, and left it in the house.

A few months later Helen was interviewing a candidate for a job when the interviewee suddenly said that they could see the spirit of a woman standing behind Helen who had said that she lived with her. The interviewee then went on to describe the cottage and even mentioned a picture that the previous owners had left behind; this was a copy of a late 1800s original which showed the landlord, George Peacock, and his daughter Ada. Helen was also told that the spirit wanted to give her a pink rose from the cottage garden.

Coincidentally the rose bush in the cottage garden blooms with just a single pink flower on one particular day, May 22nd, the birthday of Elizabeth Peacock, George's wife.

Later owners of the property believed that 'Lizzie' still lived there as she had made her presence known 'in some of the nicest ways'.

The small, thatched building stands on the opposite side of the B660 to the Blacksmith's Arms public house.

Grid reference: TL06575441

Thurleigh Road

This is another tale which may have got a bit confused with the passage of time.

On the road to Thurleigh from Ravensden, along Gray's Hill, a ghostly coach, pulled by four ghostly horses, has been seen. The coach is said to drive from Wood End to Thrayles End Farm where the moat of an old manor is said to still exist.

There are a couple of problems with this one. Firstly I can't find Thrayles End Farm, the nearest being Traylesfield Farm, but this isn't near the Thurleigh to Ravensden road. A second point is that the road from Ravensden to Thurleigh runs up a valley and not along Gray's Hill, but to the left of the road, just before Wood End, is a hill on top of which is Gray's Hill Farm. The road which runs along that hill past the farm is called Graze Hill. If you head south along Graze Hill you meet the B660. Keep going and after a few hundred metres the B660 turns hard right and in front is a track which leads to Mowsbury Hill complete with moat (in the middle of a golf course). From Wood End to Traylesfield Farm the road rises twenty metres to virtually the top of Graze Hill (an alternative spelling of Gray's?), then turns sharp left to go back downhill towards the moat at Mowsbury Hill. This looks like the most likely candidate for the site, which is the location given by the grid reference below. In fact, it seems that the whole area is called Ravensden, including the part on the map called Cleat Hill where the B660 heads towards Mowbury Hill.

Another possibility is that, as Traylesfield and Thrayles are very similar, then Thrayles End could have been along the Thurleigh road north of Wood End and east of Traylesfield. This would then place the site closer to grid reference: TL058561. The only problem with this theory is that there is no sign of a moat in that area, though it may have been obliterated years ago (over one hundred years ago, as the only moat in the area on the 1886 map is again at Mowsbury Hill).

Grid reference: TL057545

RISELEY

Riseley lies to the north of the county and is a large village with a population of 1270. The village is a mixture of old and new housing as it has grown considerably in the last few years. Nonetheless the High Street is still lined with timber framed houses and thatched cottages.

Buryfields Farm

In the 1950s Buryfields Farm was occupied by Ken Surridge and his family. The farm turned out to be one of the most haunted sites in the district. Lamps would light up of their own accord, a pump collapsed hurting one of his daughters, and two of his children would wake up in the night terrified. The reason for the terror was that his daughter once saw a door and a dark figure where there should have been a solid wall. The outside doors caused the greatest problems, as even when properly locked they would open during the night. Ken even drove six inch nails into one door but by the morning the door was open, with the nails still in place. The family dog hated going into the farmhouse.

Ken said that the haunting was more a feeling of a presence than anything tangible. A stockman, who was in a field nearby, heard screams emanating from the servants' quarters. A terrified girl told him she had seen a menacing man, but the stockman could find nothing.

Grid reference: TL05356104

Church Lane

In the late 1970s a local family were walking down Church Lane late at night. As they looked towards the church they saw that it was in ruins and they could see straight through to the altar. This was odd as the church is still not in ruins to this day.

Grid reference: TL03936303

Eastfields Corner

Ken Surridge, of Buryfields Farm (see the entry above), was travelling along the road towards the village of Dean when he suddenly became aware of a sound like a horse approaching rapidly. Next second he heard it as it plunged through the hedgerow next to him and galloped across the road from one side to the other. The only thing was that, during all of the time that he heard the sounds of the horse, nothing at all was visible.

There were two other witnesses present at the time of the encounter and all three said that they felt the cold air as it raced past them and they could all hear the sounds that it made, but nothing could be seen.

Grid reference: TL04396587

The Fox and Hounds

The Fox and Hounds public house is haunted by the ghost of a nurse. The ghost pursues the usual practices of turning lights on and off, and making the sound of footsteps overhead. In addition an occasional ghostly cough has been heard. Her favourite haunt is the fireplace in the lounge, but she has also been seen crossing the car park. It is said that the nurse died when she was run over by a coach as she crossed the road. As happens so often in history, her body was taken into the nearest public house, in this case the Fox and Hounds, but it seems that only her mortal remains left.

Grid reference: TL03976266

Tom Knocker's Pond

Tom Knocker's pond lies just over two kilometres south of Riseley on the east side of the road to Bletsoe. The area is alleged to be haunted by the spirit of someone who drowned there many years ago.

Grid reference: TL03076059

ROXTON

Roxton lies in the centre of a market gardening area encompassing Wyboston, Chawston and Colesden. It has a population of 1,190.

Roxton has a very unusual Congregational church which was built in 1808. Most churches have either a tiled roof or a roof covered in lead but the Roxton church is thatched. Nearby stands Roxton House which is a red-bricked Georgian country house set amidst parkland. At the edge of the park lies the Lodge, a pretty thatched building on the main road.

The Chequers Inn

The Chequers Inn was haunted by a ghost the residents had named Mabel. She showed her presence by turning on the bathroom taps, turning off the beer pumps and even turning off the water at the mains. A few years ago the 'Bedford Record' ran a report about noises in the pub that had disturbed the landlord. He had heard the sounds of furniture being moved around during the night and had at first thought it was a burglar (a rather noisy one). Eventually he realised that it was Mabel making the noise.

Occasionally there had been sightings of a white figure in the bar and in the cottage next door. It is believed that the pub was once a private house and that the cottage next door was the servant's quarters. There is a sad story associated with the house of a maid servant who fell in love with the squire's son and became pregnant. When he found out he murdered her. The pub is now, once again, a private house.

Grid reference: TL15255439

SANDY

Sandy is an ancient town with a population of 10,660. It strategically lies where the Ivel Valley cuts through the Greensand Ridge with evidence of two Iron Age hill forts, Caesar's Camp and Galley Hill. The Romans were also present in Sandy with a settlement along the road which ran from Baldock to Godmanchester. Roman burials, rare sculpture and other artefacts have been found in the area.

In 1870 a mansion was built just off the Potton to Sandy road for Arthur Wellesley Peel. Arthur was the youngest son of Sir Robert Peel the Prime Minister and founder of the police force. The Lodge is now the home of the Royal Society for the Protection of Birds (RSPB) and is surrounded by a nature reserve complete with hides.

Potton Road

In 1997 a lady called Michelle was being driven to night school at Sandy Upper School by her friend Andy. They were travelling down the B1042 and had passed the entrance to the RSPB bird sanctuary at about seven o'clock. This area of road is heavily wooded and hence dark so the driver had his main headlights on. As they drove downhill into a left hand bend a figure suddenly appeared on there left and proceeded to cross the road. The driver had no time to react as they were so close, but there was no accident as the car drove straight through the figure.

Michelle described the apparition as being the headless figure of a skinny woman with a big chest. She was dressed in modern attire and wearing trousers. Michelle also noted that at the woman's feet trotted a small dog, the size of a Jack Russell terrier.

Grid reference: TL18714863

SEGENHOE

Segenhoe has always been a small place with few inhabitants and dominated by Segenhoe Manor and the church of All Saints. It is effectively part of Ridgmont which was the birthplace of the Countess of Strathmore, the late Queen Mother, and mother to the present Queen Elizabeth.

Segenhoe was the original Saxon village and it was renamed Ridgemont (*Rougemont*) after the Norman conquest of 1066.

All Saints

This ruined church is located just off the Segenhoe Manor Road, which lies to the left of the Eversholt Road about six hundred metres from the A507, south-west of the centre of Ridgmont. The church was built in the eleventh century close to Segenhoe cum Ridgmont (on the map this is labelled as Segenhoe Manor). The church was adapted over the centuries so that it includes architecture from the eleventh up to the nineteenth centuries. In the end the church suffered from structural problems making it uneconomical to repair and it was finally decommissioned and a new church built in nearby Ridgmont. The old church started to decay and was going to be demolished but Bedfordshire County Council bought it in 1982. Even though the church itself is no longer in use the site is still used for burials.

There is no reported haunting of the church and its surroundings but one paranormal group, who investigated the site, did report "Within 10-15 minutes I witnessed a flash of light that kept appearing at the top of a pillar and moving quite rapidly across the width of the church, this happened about 3-4 times."

Grid reference: SP98113580

SEWELL

The attractive little hamlet of Sewell can be found on the other side of the A5 to Houghton Regis. Now the area is dominated by old chalk quarry workings and the former Dunstable to Leighton Buzzard railway line. The extensive earthworks of the Iron Age fortress of Maiden Bower can be found at the top of the downs, just a few hundred metres to the south of Sewell.

Sewell Cutting

In 1988 the 'Bedfordshire Magazine' ran an article on an unusual photograph. A young man and his family were taking a walk through

Sewell Cutting on the old Dunstable to Leighton Buzzard railway line. As with any family on a day out, he was taking pictures of the area, now a nature reserve. When the film was developed there appeared a picture of a young woman in 1930s style dress standing in front of a railway carriage window. The young man recalls that he did not take such a picture in the area and neither did any member of his family. The company who developed the film insist that a picture could not have been accidentally included from someone else's film.

The road to Sewell lies to the north of Dunstable, on the left as you pass through the chalk cutting at the edge of the town (grid reference: TL00302353). Follow this new road past the houses until, after a sharp left turn, you reach the railway bridge. Pass under the bridge and turn left up the hill and continue for about two hundred metres until you reach the level of the old railway line (now part of a long distance cycle path). I suggest you park near the bridge and walk up the hill, as it is usually very muddy and deeply rutted by other vehicles.

Grid reference: SP995227

SILSOE

Silsoe lies just off the A6 south of Clophill and has a population of 1,660. The village has a quiet high street (now that it has been bypassed) lined with old buildings. Nearby is Wrest Park Gardens which are amongst the finest in the country and managed by English Heritage. The formal gardens were initially laid out in 1710 then modified by 'Capability' Brown in 1760. The gardens abound with historic buildings and ornaments.

Ampthill Road

A house in Ampthill Road was haunted by the ghost of a little girl. 'Luton News' once interviewed Mrs. 'Mabs' Manby in 1987 when she had been living at the house for twenty-five years with her husband Dave. "I do often see it cross the hall, it's a small white figure." One of her friends had also seen the ghost and is reported to have said "Something has just flitted across your hall." Mrs. Manby said that she sees the ghost two or three times a year and that she is unconcerned about her little 'guest'.

The house in question, 'Silsoe House', is believed to have once been lived in by the estate agent to the de Grey family, the owners of Wrest Park.

Over a hundred years ago the house was lived in by Mrs. Hallam and, at the time, Bill Turner was lodging with her while he was working on her garden. One night he heard a faint tapping on the door of the next bedroom; this was followed by silence then a creaking on the stairs. This happened six times then, as Bill was settling down to sleep, he felt something brush his bed. Leaping out of bed he lit a lamp and could hear the floorboards creaking outside his bedroom. When he investigated he was shocked to see a small, fair-haired girl wearing a pinafore and no shoes, or stockings. The child was obviously in distress as she ran past him and disappeared by the bed. The following morning another lodger asked "Who was the little girl I saw on the landing last night? She tapped on my door, and when I answered it, she just faded away into the shadows of the staircase." Mrs. Hallam said that her name was Sarah and that she had lived in the house about thirty years ago with her father and stepmother. Sarah was looked after by a nurse who she was devoted to but unfortunately the nurse was dismissed. Sarah was distraught and it is said she pined away and died. A previous owner of the house had said that the little girl appeared to him quite often and that she was looking for the nurse.

Grid reference: TL08123582

The Old George

The ghost of Lady Elizabeth Grey is said to haunt the Old George in Silsoe. The landlord, John Bridge, reported that he had never seen or heard her but people staying at the inn say they had heard footsteps. John's only experience was when he once went to his bedroom and felt as if there was a strange presence there, but he could not describe what or who it was.

In 1959 the then landlady of the Old George had so many problems with the ghost that she called in an exorcist. A psychical research group

duly arrived but there was no evidence of the ghost (until after they had left). At that time the ghost kept slamming doors in the early hours of the morning which began to tell on the landlady.

In 1960 a man doing some repairs in the Old George inn looked up to see the figure of a woman dressed in grey go past. He described her as a young woman with a large picture hat. The hat was obviously so remarkable that he completely neglected to note anything else about the apparition other than that she wore grey.

Lady Elizabeth Grey was a member of the de Grey family who had been the owners of Wrest Park for nearly seven hundred years. Elizabeth was a great and beautiful lady who met and fell in love with the young coachman at the Old George inn in Silsoe. Knowing her father would never approve of such a liaison, she hid out in the Old George (then called simply the George Inn) with her lover while her father scoured the countryside all around looking for her.

For two weeks she managed to hide away from her father. Eventually though she learnt that her location had been discovered and that her father was on the way to fetch her. The lovers decided to escape and set off in a coach at reckless speed. So great was their haste that the young coach driver took a corner too fast and the coach turned over into a lake where Elizabeth, who was trapped inside, drowned. Nothing is known of the fate of the coachman, Elizabeth's lover. Elizabeth then returned to haunt the inn where she had stayed for those two weeks.

One other strange thing about the Old George was that, during some renovation work being carried out in 1992, workmen opened up the fireplace in the lounge bar and found an old gravestone at the back. Nothing was visible on the stone except for the word 'widow' and there is nothing to say why it was located there, another incident lost in the mists of time.

The ghost is a bit quieter now as with many such instances the ghosts fade after a hundred years or so. The last reported incidences were the feeling of a presence and the sound of footsteps, but this was over ten years ago.

Grid reference: TL08153585

SOMERIES

Someries can be found just south of Luton, literally right next to Luton airport. A brick building, Someries castle, was built on the site by Sir John Wenlock in the fifteenth century. Now all that visibly remains are a few ruins and some earthworks which are open to the public all year round.

The only remaining building is the gatehouse to the original manor house. All that remains of the manor is an earthwork with the clearly defined outline of the manor. Bricks were taken from the manor to build the nearby farm houses in the seventeenth century.

Someries Castle

The ghost of Sir John Lord Wenlock has been seen in the grounds of Someries Castle. Sir John was a soldier who first fought for Henry VI at St. Albans in 1455. Later he joined the Earl of Salisbury and supported the House of York. In 1471 he joined the Earl of Warwick and the Duke of Clarence.

As an experienced solder he was placed in charge of a division at the battle of Tewkesbury. During the battle the Duke of Somerset had tried a daring manoeuvre which would have succeeded if Wenlock had supported him. The ensuing rout left Somerset livid and he challenged Wenlock over the matter, remembering that Wenlock had changed sides several times during the Wars of the Roses. Wenlock accused Somerset of being a novice and asked why he should have supported a doomed operation? Somerset was so angry he struck Wenlock with his poleaxe and dashed out his brains. Wenlock was seventy-one when he died on the fourth day of May 1471 and he was buried in Someries Chapel.

Grid reference: TL11882012

STANBRIDGE

Stanbridge is a small village between Dunstable and Leighton Buzzard with a population of 720. There is a green in the centre of the village with an inn at one end and the parish church of St. John the Baptist at the other. The church is mediaeval but was largely restored in the late nineteenth century. It contains an Elizabethan octagonal pulpit and an Early English font.

Station Road

On the 12th October 1979, at nine thirty in the evening, twenty-six year old carpet fitter Roy Fulton was returning home after playing in a darts match in Leighton Buzzard. He was driving along Station Road in Stanbridge and had reached the junction with Peddars Lane when he saw a young man, about twenty years of age, wearing dark trousers, a jumper and white open necked shirt, thumbing a lift. Mr. Fulton stopped short of the man and watched as he walked towards his Mini van. The man

opened the passenger door and got in without saying a word, he didn't even speak when Mr. Fulton asked where he was going. The man simply raised his arm and indicated the direction of Totternhoe and Dunstable.

After about a mile the car was doing forty miles per hour and the man had still not uttered a word. Mr. Fulton decided to offer his passenger a cigarette so he turned round to look at the man and was alarmed to discover that there was no one there. Understandably shocked, Mr. Fulton rapidly stopped the car and checked the back seat; there was no sign of his passenger.

Mr. Fulton later described the man as very solid and totally real and he had no reason to think that he wasn't alive. He described the man's complexion as pale with a rather long face which was topped off by a crop of short, dark, curly hair. According to Mr. Fulton there was no way that the man could have got out of the car as they were doing forty miles per hour at the time. When the man had first gotten into the car the interior light had come on; between then and when he disappeared the light remained off, so the passenger door was never opened. All of the above events happened in the span of a few minutes.

The matter was reported to the police (after Mr. Fulton had been for a stiff drink) who sent out a patrol car, but there was no sign of the young man. According to 'The Dunstable Gazette' of 18th October a young man had been killed on the road where Mr. Fulton picked up his passenger. It was said that he was killed by a drunk driver returning from a party; though a search of old newspaper articles for several years back produced no such report.

Grid reference: SP96592375

STEVINGTON

There has been a settlement at Stevington since Saxon times. The largely stone-built village has a post mill that was in operation until 1936. It was purchased by Bedfordshire County Council in 1951 and restored, so that now it would work if it wasn't for the lightning conductor. In the boundary wall of the churchyard is Holywell, which was a pilgrimage site in the Middle Ages as the well had the power to cure eye afflictions. I found the water to be cold and refreshing, and with an interesting taste, probably due to its having filtered down through the graveyard.

The Cross

In a house near the cross in the centre of the village there once lived a man who was a true miser, hoarding every bit of money that he had. When he became ill he was rushed to hospital where he unfortunately died. Now it seems he has returned to the house in ghostly form to search for his money.

You may not be able to take it with you, but this man will certainly give it a good try.

Grid reference: SP989532

St. Mary the Virgin

Around the church, dedicated to St. Mary the Virgin, a shadowy figure complete with large hat and cape has been seen (described as being straight off a Sandemans Port bottle).

Grid reference: SP99045362

STOTFOLD

Fairfield Hospital

Mary was a new nurse who was spending her first night on the geriatric ward at Fairfield Hospital. Part way through her shift she went off to the kitchen to make everyone drinks, then realised she had forgotten one of the orders. She called through the hatch "did you want tea or coffee?" and a voice replied "Tea, with two sugars." Mary was very surprised when the nurse, whose drink Mary couldn't remember, appeared a few moments later and said she wanted coffee with one sugar. She had heard Mary call but could not make out the words, so she had come to the kitchen to find out what she wanted. There were no other people around and the nurse had not passed anyone on the way to the kitchen. On other occasions Mary was in the kitchen alone when the door handle started moving. Each time she looked there was no one to be seen in the corridor; no matter how quickly she opened the door.

Another nurse, Jenny Butterworth, had worked at Fairfield hospital for fifteen years and remembered vividly many of her paranormal experiences there. A few months after she first started work she had to move a wheelchair from the dining area to a dormitory. When she returned with another wheelchair the first had moved fifteen feet away by a partition. She was puzzled as to how this had happened but thought little of it and moved the two chairs back together. This was at seven o'clock in the morning and the start of her shift. When she returned, shortly after, both chairs had been moved far apart with no sound being made. She thought an assistant was playing tricks on her but when she enquired she was told she would "soon get used to this sort of thing happening".

One day, as she was walking down the drive to work, she saw one of the domestic staff, wearing an unmistakable green uniform, in front of

her. When she next looked the figure had disappeared, but there was nowhere for them to have gone.

Whilst on night duty one winter's night in 1990 Jenny and a male colleague heard the sounds of heavy, dragging feet coming from an empty bedroom. They were reluctant to investigate but their duty said that they had to...the room was empty. This sound became a regular occurrence an hour after midnight.

One evening in 1993 Jenny had to take a patient to the Lister Hospital in Stevenage. When she returned, it was two o'clock in the morning. Whilst in reception the sliding window suddenly opened by itself. When the night receptionist, Fred, walked in she told him what had happened and he said that it was the ghost. To demonstrate he told her to put her keys on the counter, then he went off to answer a telephone call. Jenny looked away for a few seconds and when she turned back her keys were gone. When Fred returned he showed her where they were, in the correct place on the key rack. Fred told her that there was always someone sitting there who can only be seen by some people and not by others.

On a winter's night in 1996 all the patients had been settled and all the doors and windows were locked. The next second a security guard arrived to say that all the doors and windows had been opened. Jenny and the guard went and relocked them all, but later that night he returned to say they were open again.

Jenny only encountered two apparitions in her fifteen years at Fairfield. The first has already been mentioned. The second was when she was chatting with a nursing officer, Christine, at one thirty in the morning. They looked over towards a hedge and saw a male figure in a heavy coat. They both thought it was a colleague, Peter, but then decided it wasn't, especially when they looked again and he had vanished, again with nowhere to hide.

Again on a night shift Jenny heard a patient call out "Nurse, can I have a bedpan?" Jenny thought this was strange because that particular patient was badly disfigured and rarely spoke. On checking, Jenny found the patient was fast asleep. In another incidence Jenny heard a patient cry out, followed by a loud thud. She rushed to the bed thinking a patient had fallen out, only to find that the bed in question was empty. The nursing sister told Jenny that this occurred every night.

In 1997 a young ambulance driver called Nikki made her first visit to Fairfield, at night. She was there to transfer a patient, so she went into the hospital, taking a wheelchair with her. When she got inside she realised that she would actually need a stretcher, so she returned to the ambulance. When she got back outside she found that the ambulance had moved fifteen feet across the car park. This was in spite of the fact that the engine was turned off, the keys were with Nikki, the handbrake was on and the car park was virtually level.

Fairfield hospital was originally opened in 1860 and called 'The Three Counties Asylum'. The first patients moved in on 12th March 1860. From that point on the asylum grew as the population increased until there were one thousand inmates. In the 1980s more and more patients were transferred to Care in the Community schemes and the hospital slowly emptied until the doors of Fairfield finally closed in 1998.

Today the 27.6 hectare site is becoming one enormous housing development (Fairfield Park) and the original main building of the hospital (built in 1856 and now listed as Grade II) is being converted into one and two bedroom apartments (Fairfield Hall).

Grid reference: TL203351

STUDHAM

Studham is the most southerly village in Bedfordshire and has a population of 1,180. In the Domesday Book of 1086 it is given as *Estodham,* which means a homestead where horses are kept.

The Blue Man

One of the strangest tales that has come from Bedfordshire must be that of the Blue Man of Studham. Not necessarily a ghost story, but interesting nonetheless.

The events took place on 28th January 1967 in a small dell near to Studham Lower School. Seven boys from the school were returning there after lunch, at about 1-45pm, when they encountered the Blue Man.

TOWNS AND VILLAGES

Ten year old Alex Butler was the first to see him/her/it, as he was a little ahead of the others as they approached the dell. Climbing the surrounding bank he looked down into the dell and saw the Blue Man, not twenty metres away. The figure was described as a little blue man with a beard and wearing a tall hat. Alex called to his friends and they all rushed over and stared down into the dell. At first they were too amazed to move, but after a while they all ran down into the dell towards the figure. The man did not move, instead he seemed to emit a cloud of yellowish-blue mist, then he quite literally vanished.

The boys searched the dell but at first there was no sign of the Blue Man. Then he was spotted further along the bank, again about twenty metres away. As the boys moved towards him he once again vanished in a mist. They all reached the spot where he had been standing, but there was again no sign of him. To their surprise he was seen once more standing near to where he had first been spotted.

As they stood staring at him they became aware of a noise, which they described as "voices not like a human". The noises seemed to be coming from an area close to the boys. The next instant they heard the sound of the whistle denoting the end of lunch at the school, and they all rushed off to tell their teacher what they had seen.

From the boys' description the man appeared to be about a metre tall, with a hat or helmet about sixty centimetres high and which had a rounded top. He had two round eyes, a triangle for a nose and was wearing a one-piece outfit with a broad black belt, at the front of which was a black box about fifteen centimetres square. It seems that his beard was split into two below his chin and ran down each side of his chest. The boys also said that the man's arms remained at his side all the time they were looking at him, but they could not describe his feet and legs as they looked 'misty'.

People are convinced that the boys were telling the truth, especially as the tale seemed too detailed to have been invented by them. So what was he, an alien or something preternatural?

Grid reference: TL022156

SUTTON

Sutton consists of one street and is a small village that was given to the Burgoyne family by John o' Gaunt. The Burgoynes lived in the village until the family died out just before the Second World War. The village contains an excellent example of a mediaeval packhorse bridge, and a ford.

Old Manor House

Two Cavaliers were at the Old Manor House in Sutton when the Roundheads arrived. They tried to escape through a tunnel which connected the house to the church (and possibly beyond) but, unfortunately for the Cavaliers, it seems the Roundheads knew of the passage and were waiting for the men as they exited. The Cavaliers were caught, executed and now their ghosts haunt the area.

Evidence that the passageway existed was provided by a deep hole which appeared one day in Sutton Park ("big enough to take a cow"). Sutton Park lies on the opposite side of the church to that where the manor stood. In addition part of a tunnel was found when the church was being repaired. Unfortunately this tunnel was sealed up, as it was felt to be unsafe.

Grid reference: TL220472

THURLEIGH

Thurleigh lies to the north of the county and has a population of 640. The village is a small compact one with groups of picturesque thatched, timber-framed cottages. The church of St. Peter has a twelfth century tower and stands next to the remains of a mediaeval motte and bailey castle.

To the north lies Thurleigh airfield used by the United States during the Second World War and later by the Defence Research Establishment. Part of the airfield is now a business park.

Keysoe Road

Keysoe Road has its share of ghosts, all related to the time when it was the administrative quarters used by the 306th Bombardment Group of the US Air Force. Later the site became an RAF officer's mess.

In the early 90s, Michael Cook was living in the mess whilst working for the Defence Research Agency at Thurleigh airfield. Whilst staying there, he would often hear the sounds of footsteps outside his door after he had gone to bed. Every time he investigated he found that there was no one there. When he talked about it with the other residents of the mess, he was told that the mess was haunted by an American airman.

One evening Michael was in the reading room. He watched, fascinated, as the entrance door to the room slowly opened, then just as slowly closed all by itself. The hairs stood up on the back of his neck.

Early in 1991 there was a heavy fall of snow which forced Michael to stay in the mess over the weekend. Now entirely alone he was sitting in the reading room when a light bulb suddenly dropped out of the socket. It fell onto the coffee table just a few inches from his hand. Michael said that it bounced without breaking When he had recovered from the shock he felt a very strong sense of someone else's presence in the room.

Grid reference: TL05695907

Thurleigh Airfield

The airfield was occupied by the 306th Bombardment Group of the United States Air Force during the Second World War and the ghosts which haunt the site are related to that era. Eventually the site became part of the Royal Aircraft Establishment and because of this it was regularly patrolled by Ministry of Defence policemen and dogs.

Patrols had repeatedly reported seeing wartime aircrew playing cards in a lighted hut. When they went round to the door to investigate they found the hut deserted and in darkness. One policeman, on patrol with his dog, spotted a man on a bicycle in the half-light of evening. The cyclist turned off towards a hanger, so the policeman went round the other way

to cut him off. But search where he might, he could find no sign of the man or the bicycle. John Ziarkos, who was a crew chief at the airfield during World War Two, identified the cyclist as a young airman who had killed himself during the war.

This particular airman had always been convinced that every time he went on a mission he was going to die. But his prediction did not come true and instead he survived every mission until, tragically, he finally used a gun to take his own life.

Grid reference: TL049603

TIDBURY

Tidbury lies just to the south of Riseley and was originally a farm, which was later swallowed up by the Royal Aircraft Establishment. The original site of the farm now occupies a corner of Thurleigh airfield.

Tidbury Farm

This area is, or should I say was, haunted by the Tidbury ghost. A local resident, Eric Hancock, was out late one night when he saw a ghostly white figure. Eric stood transfixed as it crossed the road in front of him. Once across the road it started to walk over the fields in the direction of Tidbury Farm but it never reached there, as it suddenly vanished.

The farm has since been swallowed up by the Royal Aircraft Establishment and no recent sightings have been reported. There is, however, one path within the site that seems to make the guard dogs' hackles rise.

The original farm lay at grid reference: TL043606, right in the middle of what was to become the airfield's runways. It is most likely that the ghost crossed the road which ran from just north of Galsey Wood (on the left of the Riseley to Bletsoe Road) to Backnoe End and Whitwick Green. The latter was also swallowed by the airfield and only Whitwickgreen Farm now remains. The road no longer exists, but its route is still marked by the parish boundary.

Grid reference: TL040605

TODDINGTON

Toddington is a large village five kilometres to the north of Houghton Regis in the south of the county. It has a current population of 4,820. Toddington has a large village green with an impressive cruciform church dedicated to St. George. The town's wealth came from the straw plait industry and is reflected in the number of fine buildings that surround the green.

To the east of the church lies the mound of a mediaeval motte and bailey castle called Conger Hill. Toddington Manor lies to the north-west and is mainly nineteenth century in origin, but it does contain evidence of an earlier mansion where Queen Elizabeth I once stayed. The manor gardens are occasionally open to the general public.

The Bedford Arms

The Bedford Arms is supposed to be haunted by a nautical ghost. In the winter of 1999 the Phantom Realm Society investigated the pub and declared that it was haunted. The landlords at that time, Richard and Nicky Bollen, said that they had never seen anything themselves but the pub did have a long history of being haunted.

Regulars have reported seeing a man in the fireplace, being tapped on the shoulder, and hearing the sound of footsteps. The ghost is said to be that of a sea captain who returned home to find his wife and child murdered. He continued to live at the cottage for a while but was so overcome with grief that he eventually hung himself from a rafter in what is now a bedroom. A priest was called in to exorcise the pub but the ghost is still being seen by locals and members of the landlords' family, both in the bar and the bedrooms.

Helen Barlow, who worked in the pub, said that at night the ghost walked down the passage upstairs and you could hear his footsteps. She usually only saw his head and shoulders and described him as a large man with a beard. She has only seen him fully once and believes he was wearing a red and blue tunic with an elaborate belt. A previous landlady, Marianne Steele, saw him standing by the fireplace in the smaller bar and described him as a Cavalier. Could there be two ghosts, as a Cavalier could not easily be mistaken for a sea captain? One night the bar bell gave two distinct rings though there was no one there to have rung it.

Grid reference: TL00912858

The Bell

The Bell is haunted by a ghost that is heard but it has never been seen. Four years ago the landlord, Marcus Hayden, was having some work done on a bedroom. Woodworm had been found in the floorboards, so they had to be replaced and the remaining original timbers treated to prevent a further attack. As is usually the case, any alteration starts the poltergeist activity. At four o'clock in the afternoon the carpenter left and shortly afterwards Marcus heard an "almighty bang" from the empty room. This was followed shortly after by another bang. Marcus rushed upstairs and checked the room but found nothing. The door and window had been left open for ventilation because of the chemicals being used, yet now the door was shut. The door has a latch which has to be pressed

down to close the door and it swings naturally open, yet it had closed. Marcus opened the door and went back downstairs, then five minutes later there was another almighty bang. Marcus by now was fed up, so he rushed upstairs, stood in the middle of the room and told the ghost to stop as the alterations were necessary and he was only trying to improve the pub. It seems that Marcus' pleas did not fall on deaf ears, as the banging did indeed stop.

In November 2002 Tess, the assistant manager for ten years, had an uncomfortable night at the pub. Her husband got up at five in the morning to go to work and they heard the sounds of creaking boards and doors banging in empty rooms. One of the back rooms is always icy cold, irrespective of the weather. Downstairs Hazel, one of the bar staff, has felt a ghostly hand on her shoulder. This has also been felt in the room Marcus had had repaired. Customers have also reported seeing a ghostly woman sitting on a stool in the corner of the bar. A former landlord had told Tess that one night he felt the sheets on his bed being pulled tight so he couldn't move. He asked whatever was doing it to stop and, fortunately, it did.

Rumour has it that a young girl was once imprisoned in a bedroom upstairs and now that same room is plagued by poltergeist activity including glasses being broken.

Grid reference: TL00932891

M1 Junction 12

Several accidents seem to have happened on the M1 by Junction 12 at Toddington but not all of them are due to bad driving, as some may have a more supernatural cause.

Many of the drivers have reported seeing a man dressed in dark clothing who is seen wandering around in front of their cars, so that they have had to swerve to avoid hitting him. When they look back there is never any sign of the man and the drivers are left wondering if it wasn't just their imagination playing tricks on them.

Grid reference: TL020298

The Sow and Pigs

The ghost that appears in the Sow and Pigs haunts a very strange and inconvenient area. Customers making use of the facilities in the gents' toilet get the fright of their lives when he appears next to them and calmly asks them to "move over". This tends to put the customer off what he was doing and has led to one or two little accidents!

Grid reference: TL00952894

WILDEN

Wilden is a scattered community to the north of Bedford. It was mentioned in the Domesday Book as *Wildene*. It consists of 160 homes in a largely rural area with plenty of agriculture.

The local church, St. Nicholas, has been well maintained and has been dated to 1231. Next to the village green there is a school that has been in existence for four hundred years.

Manor Farm House

There are several ghosts associated with Wilden Manor Farm House. Recently the ghost of a woman has been seen walking into the now derelict house. Screams have also been heard on the site; these have been associated with a horse rider who fell into a ditch and was killed.

Many people have witnessed stones being thrown from the area

around the house, some of which have reached the garden of the Victoria Arms pub opposite (grid reference: TL09495521). Stones have even been said to have reached the churchyard which is one hundred metres away. People who visited the site have heard the sound of stones hitting an old caravan which lies alongside the path. A phantom fire which originated near the gate by the road (on a line between the house and the pub) and grew till it was nearly two metres across, was once seen. It has also been reported that stones have been seen hovering in the air even in broad daylight. A taxi driver was waiting for his fare in the gateway to the house with the engine off. Suddenly the windscreen wipers started operating and the fuel gauge needle started to flick up and down by itself.

The house is a timber framed building and dates from the seventeenth century and is listed as Grade II. According to a legend handed down from a hundred years ago a witch was burned alive on the track leading to the manor. On the track there are two old caravans which, it is said, were occupied by two gypsy brothers. One died of cancer and the other died a week later of 'causes unknown'. Another story says that the house was cursed by an unknown lady.

I have had a talk with the owner of Manor Farm whose family has farmed the site for five generations and the results were not as expected. Neither the farmer nor any member of his family has experienced anything in or around the house. What is also interesting is that the original source of many of the occurrences above did not have permission to enter the farmer's land and had never even talked to the farmer until recently. How can you research a site without getting background data from the owner (present or past)? And worst of all what were people doing entering his land without his permission? Any true investigator would always get permission to investigate a site before entering it! Oh! And the caravan was occupied by the first member of the present farmer's family to own the land. When he bought the land in 1954 Manor Farm House was already dilapidated, even though the previous owner had been living there. The new owner lived at the pub for a while, then moved to the caravan to save money. Most of the sightings, and other phenomena, are associated with one man who has studied the site, so it is possible that he is the cause, by way of poltergeist activity. People have also been responsible for some of the instances of stone throwing (mainly to scare unwelcome visitors off). So is the site haunted or is it purely the result of human activity?

Grid reference: TL09485534

Ravensden Road

The Ravensden Road runs between Wilden and Ravensden and is haunted by the ghost of a witch. A local tale says that a bride and groom saw the witch as they passed though Wilden about seventy years ago. She wore a black bonnet beneath which her features were coarse and masculine. She turned her head towards the bride and gave her a malevolent glare.

In 1873 Mrs. Goodall and her daughter were travelling along the road in a pony and trap in broad daylight. They saw a figure walking along the grass verge in long black trailing garments. They too were subjected to the glare before the figure disappeared. Later the Goodalls described the figure as 'fiendish', with a coarse and ugly face which appeared almost masculine. When Mrs. Goodall made enquiries about the area, she was told that the stretch of road in question had long had a reputation for being haunted. A representative of the Society for Psychical Research interviewed the two women and declared that their sighting was genuine.

A Wilden man, who saw the apparition much later, said that she appeared to glide rather than walk. This happened in 1973 and is the last recorded sighting. The event took place in broad daylight and the man was so shaken that he had to stop off at the pub for a 'stiff drink'.

The local people believe she is the ghost of Mother Sutton, a witch who terrorised the neighbourhood and was eventually hanged along with her daughter in 1612. She earned her living looking after hogs until she quarrelled with a local farmer. She is alleged to have put a spell on his pigs so that they became squealing, hysterical animals. Another version of the tale simply states that she was a witch, who was put out of her house and died of exposure on the roadside.

Grid reference: TL082549

WILLINGTON

Willington lies to the south of the River Ouse on a loop off the Bedford to Sandy road. It has a population of 760, with the oldest part of the village lying closest to the loop road.

The church of St. Lawrence was built in the sixteenth century, most likely by Sir John Gostwick who was an official of Cardinal Wolsey and who later held high office under Henry VIII.

Sir John acquired the Manor of Willington in 1529 and built a manor house where Henry VIII was reported to have stayed. The manor has virtually disappeared but the Tudor Dovecote and stables still remain. The

dovecote is a massive stone structure with nesting boxes for one and a half thousand birds and is now managed by The National Trust.

Willington Manor

Though a ghost has never been seen at Willington Manor, it has revealed itself in other ways. There have been numerous reported incidents of heavy footsteps being heard and the sound of a bell. Dogs are particularly upset by the ghost, especially in the early hours of the morning.

The identity of the ghost is unknown and there appears to be no reason for the haunting. The only possible connection was when the skeleton of a man was found bricked up in a wall whilst the house was being rebuilt early in the twentieth century.

Willington Manor has been in existence since before the time of Henry VIII. Over the centuries two major fires and consequent rebuilding have left the manor with a mainly Georgian façade. The house is known to have been occupied by Sir John Gostwick, Master of Hounds to King Henry in the sixteenth century. More recently the manor was occupied by the former Secretary of State for Foreign Affairs, Sir Joseph Godber.

Grid reference: TL10514981

WOBURN

Woburn still retains much of the character of a Georgian town and is acknowledged as one of the most important historical towns in the country. The whole of the main street (George Street and Bedford Street) is lined with houses from the eighteenth and nineteenth centuries.

In the centre of the town is the old Town Hall (on the left side of the image on the next page) which is now an antiques centre. The building was designed by Edward Blore (1787 to 1879) who designed the east front of Buckingham Palace.

The parish church of St. Mary lies on the approach to Woburn Park from the town centre. This building was built of Bath stone in 1860 and

replaced the original church in Bedford Street. After 1868 the old church was only being used as a Mortuary Chapel.

The Bedford Arms

The Bedford Arms hotel (now The Inn at Woburn) featured in the 'Ampthill News' in January 1974 because of its ghosts. One of the ghosts was described by sixty-eight year old Reg Williams, the night porter. "He's dressed in a smock, has an old hat and is smoking a clay pipe; about two feet long...There's a dog, like a greyhound, by his side." The first time Reg saw the ghost the hotel was closed, as work was being done to open up an old fireplace. The man and dog sit in the fireplace and have been seen numerous times but no one knows who they are.

A more frightening ghost was that of the white lady. "This was a horrible experience, it was like a load of steam coming down, I saw it take shape and it was like a woman." The white lady has also been seen by other members of staff in the reception area. A while ago a hall porter, Mr. J. Graham, left the hotel in haste one night never to return. He was in such a hurry to leave that he left his jacket and house keys behind. So what frightened him?

Grid reference: SP94943305

The Royal Oak

The ghost that haunts the Royal Oak is felt but has never been seen. It has a bad habit of turning off the taps to the beer pumps during the night, and has even occasionally turned them off during opening hours,

much to the dismay of the customers. It also slams doors and, for some unknown reason, it likes to take flowers from their vases. It has been felt as a presence on the cellar stairs.

Grid reference: SP95003290

Woburn Abbey

Numerous ghosts haunt Woburn Abbey from phantom monks to an invisible opener of doors. The Duke of Bedford spoke of one ghost "The ghost became such a nuisance that we had to change our television room…we'd be sitting there when suddenly the handle of the door at one end of the room would turn and the door would open just as though an invisible person was coming through."

A phantom monk has appeared in the area of the Crypt. It is claimed that he was the Abbot of Woburn, Robert Hobbes, who was hanged when he opposed Henry VIII's marriage to Anne Boleyn. The oak tree from which he was hung still stands in front of the house.

A monk in a brown habit has also been seen, in what is now the sculpture gallery, during excavation work in 1971. He appeared between the pillars either side of the entrance then vanished through the door. Another ghost is a figure in Victorian dress that has been seen in the antiques centre.

Throughout the building doors open with no help from the living. One morning the Duchess found Paul Getty jumping up and down in a corridor. It transpired that another guest had complained that her bedroom door had opened by itself five times during the night so that she had to get up to close it. Getty was trying to see if vibration could have caused it to open.

The jazz musician Acker Bilk (the Great Master of the Clarinet) was staying at Woburn after judging a Dairy Queen contest. He had stayed up late talking to the Duke's son, the Marquis of Tavistock, and it was four o'clock in the morning before they finally decided to retire. They were standing outside Acker Bilk's room, the Red Room, whilst they continued to talk, when Acker noticed that the doors to the room were slowly opening on their own. Tavistock casually replied, "Oh, don't bother about that. It's just a ghost. He often wanders around. I think we have seven in all at the Abbey."

In the summerhouse can be felt the unhappy presence of the Duke's grandmother. She died at the age of sixty-four when the plane she was piloting crashed on the east coast. Her ghost is not seen but an overwhelming feeling of sadness pervades the place.

The most recent haunting is thought to be that of a manservant who served the seventh Duke. One day burglars broke into the house and nearly strangled the man to death before they locked him in a cupboard in the Masquerade Room. Once they had finished plundering the house, they threw the servant out of the window and proceeded to drown him in the lake. His ghost has never been seen but doors open for him as he passes. Witnesses have claimed that a door at one end of a room would open as if someone was walking in, then the opposite door would open in the time it would have take someone to cross the room. When this kept happening in the television room the Duke got fed up of the draughts and changed the locks, but this had little effect and the doors continued to open by themselves. Eventually the Duke decided that the only solution was to have the whole area remodelled so that the route the ghost followed became a passageway.

In the private areas of the house the Duke and Duchess noticed an uncomfortable atmosphere. Sometimes they have both felt a most disconcerting sensation as if someone had touched their faces in the night with a wet hand.

Woburn Abbey was originally founded by Cistercian monks in 1145; even before that the site was occupied by a Saxon hamlet dating back at least as far as 969. In 1547 the house was confiscated and given to Henry VIII's executor, Sir John Russell. The present house dates to 1744 and was designed by Inigo Jones and further updated a century later. At that time the fourth Duke created the park and started the world famous art and furniture collection.

Grid reference: SP966325

WOBURN SANDS

Most of Woburns Sands lies in Milton Keynes, but one part of the road to Aspley Guise (Weathercock Lane) lies in Bedfordshire.

Until about 1860 Woburn Sands did not exist, instead the area was called Hogsty End. It was in 1860 that the Victorians began to develop the area as a residential town taking its name from the nearest market town, Woburn, and the major industry, sand extraction. The sand was Fullers Earth. This is very fine yellow sand used by wool fullers to clean and whiten the wool (full is from the Anglo-Saxon word *fullian* meaning to whiten). The sand has been dug in the area since 1539, or maybe even earlier. The railway reached Woburn Sands (Hogsty End) in November 1846 and the station was created thanks to the Duke of Bedford. Most of the railway line was built over the 7th Duke's land and he wanted his own station near to Woburn Abbey; unfortunately for him Woburn Sands was the nearest point at which it could be built.

Weathercock Lane

In Weathercock Lane (once known as Aspley Lane) the sounds of galloping hooves have been heard made by a phantom man on horseback (allegedly Dick Turpin). Two lovers are said to haunt Woodfield House (known as Woodfield Villa at the end of the nineteenth century) at the top of the lane though, again, some say it is the ghost of Dick Turpin. The story seems to have no basis in truth, but was the invention of a tenant who wanted his rates reduced! A phantom white lady has also been seen at the top of the embankment (towards the Aspley Hill end of the road at grid reference: SP933357).

On the site which Woodfield House now occupies (grid reference: SP93183578) it is believed that there used to stand an inn some two hundred and fifty years ago. It was here that a double murder took place. The story has it that the inn was occupied by a girl and her father. The girl had a lover she was keeping secret from her father, knowing that he wouldn't approve. The lover would come to the inn on the nights when her father was away, but one night he returned unexpectedly. The lovers panicked and hid in a large pantry to avoid being caught by the girl's father. But it was too late as the man had been watching them through the window and in a fit of rage he locked them in the cupboard and jammed furniture against the door so they couldn't escape. It is here that they died and one legend has it that their ghosts are trying to return to the pantry. There is a second version of the legend in which the father shot both his daughter and her lover, but the overall outcome was still the same.

The legend then has it that Dick Turpin broke into the house whilst looking for somewhere to hide and discovered the bodies. Knowing he

was on to a good thing, he proceeded to blackmail the father so that he could use the premises as a safe house. The bodies were buried under the cellar floor and it is said that the girl and her lover haunted the house from that point on. A séance was held in the house in the 1960s and the ghost of the daughter, Bessie, agreed to stop the haunting.

The Dick Turpin legend continues with reports of a ghost on horse back galloping down Weathercock Lane from Aspley Hill (grid reference: SP93453568) and entering Woodfield House through a hedgerow which stands where the old inn entrance would once have stood. Sometimes just the sound of ghostly hoof-beats has been heard as Black Bess charges down the hill.

Some believe that the ghost story is a work of fiction started by Mr. Blaney Key in 1948 in an attempt to get his rates reduced as he said that the ghost devalued the property. At the Rates hearing he presented the ghost as evidence, but it was dismissed as being "devoid of merit and without point or purpose". The novelty of the story drew the media's attention and it even appeared on a BBC news bulletin. One alleged witness was a girl who had been evacuated to Woodfield during the Second World War. She claimed that she had seen the arms of the murdered girl reaching out to her from above her bed. When the judge asked her what she had eaten that night she replied "cheese sandwiches", which resulted in the court degenerating into fits of laughter and the judge rejecting the petition.

Weathercock Lane lies to the east of the A5130 about four hundred metres south of Woburn Sands railway station (starting at the Weathercock Inn and going up to Aspley Hill). Woodfield House lies on the right as you travel from the Weathercock Inn, a couple of hundred metres below Aspley Hill, where the road starts to rise upwards.

Grid reference: SP933357

WOOTTON

Wootton, like many villages in the area, had a long association with the brick-making industry. At one time most of the Marston Vale was virtually one giant brick-works, most of which has now gone. In the eighteenth century church bells were made at Wootton which went to several churches in Bedfordshire and the adjoining counties.

Wootton has grown a lot in the last thirty years but several timber-framed buildings still survive. The church of St. Mary the Virgin was built in the fourteenth century and contains two fine monuments to members of the Monoux family who died in 1685 and 1707. To the west of the church lies Wootton House, built in the late seventeenth century.

The Chequers Inn

At the Chequers Inn the ghost of a groomsman who fell beneath the wheels of a coach and lost his head is said to be responsible for glasses which fall off the shelf to the ground without breaking.

The landlords Eddie and Brenda Finch think there is more than one ghost, as bar staff have complained about seeing a vanishing customer.

They would see someone out of the corner of their eye in the snack bar but when they got there the bar was empty. It seems the figure comes though a wall where there was once an old entrance. As with a lot of ghosts he seems to have little respect for modern décor and the updated structure of a property, so that he follows a route which existed when he was alive.

Grid reference: TL00124574

Fields Road

In June 2002 Barry Waddington was driving along Fields Road in Wootton. As he came round a right-hand bend a figure appeared from nowhere directly in front of him and Barry had to slam on his brakes. As his car stopped he heard the screech of tyres, a bang and felt the impact as another car drove into him.

The woman pedestrian Barry had seen came over and asked him if he was alright. He noticed that she was wearing all black, which he thought was not very sensible seeing as it was night time and Fields Road is unlit along most of its length.

Barry ran back to check the other driver and found he was uninjured. When Barry looked back at his own car the woman had gone. Both drivers had seen her, yet she had vanished on a straight section of road and there was nowhere for her to hide.

Some time later Barry's wife was told that there had been other sightings of the woman in black on that particular stretch of road.

Grid reference: TL01524484

In Conclusion

Virtually every village and town has its ghosts and virtually every public house is filled with spirits of a kind you cannot drink. These were but a few of the hundreds that are still out there waiting to be recorded. They form part of our history and our present and are a strong connection to the past. Most stories are genuine and many are confirmed by independent witnesses, but some may just be the result of an overly active imagination; you decide.

A classic example of an event which is open to interpretation comes from Hertfordshire. The tale goes that the landlord of a local public house had closed up after the lunchtime session and had gone for a nap. Some time after falling asleep in the chair he was shocked into wakefulness when a balloon was burst in his face. This was recorded as a paranormal event but was it? I recall that some twenty odd years ago I woke up in the morning after a good night's sleep to find a large bumble bee flying straight at my face; I even recall hearing its loud buzz. I naturally ducked (as well as I could as I was in bed), then was rather surprised to find that the bee had disappeared. I searched the room but it was no longer there and the windows and doors were shut so there was nowhere for it to go. I'd had a dream which had been so vivid it seemed real. How many times have you had a dream or a nightmare and woken up feeling as you did in the dream, breathless, in a panic, frightened?

Many events could have a natural origin or could just be the product of an active imagination. Of the tales in this book I have my own opinion on their authenticity, but I will keep that to myself and allow you to make up your own minds. One thing though is for certain, try as I may I cannot explain them all away and I cannot easily account for the things I have myself seen and heard. I am convinced that many are genuine.

One thing I do know is that when I am out on an investigation with other people the things they see, hear and feel will be modified by what I tell them before we start. If I tell them the full story of a site, then they are more likely to experience something related to the tale. But is this their imagination or is it because the knowledge has opened their minds up and they are listening or looking for the subtle signs? I feel that some information should be given but not all of it and certainly not enough to make people see or hear what isn't there.

Children see things that we, as adults, do not. This is mainly due to the fact that as a child grows the adults around it tell it that things like imaginary friends do not exist, they are just products of the child's imagination. But are all such things just imagination? As we grow older we lose the ability to imagine, we are constrained by the 'norms' of society, so we conform. The things we saw as children vanish and we almost seem to lose a sense. But this does not have to happen. For some people their imaginations are so good that they can manifest an image in front of their eyes. To them such images are real; can this be the source of ghosts? Or is it that we lose our open-mindedness so we can no longer see what is really there?

Chapter 2

Black Shuck

Tales of black spectral hounds abound throughout the United Kingdom and the general opinion is that you don't really want to meet one of these on a dark night.

There have not been that many reports of these dogs in recent years but they do have a long history with the first English account appearing in the Anglo-Saxon Chronicle of 1127:

"Let no-one be surprised at the truth of what we are about to relate, for it was common knowledge throughout the whole country that immediately after his arrival [Abbot Henry of Poitou] at the Abbey of Peterborough - it was the Sunday when they sing Exurge Quare o, D - many men both saw and heard a great number of huntsmen hunting. The huntsmen were black, huge and hideous, and rode on black horses and on black he-goats and their hounds were jet black with eyes like saucers and horrible. This was seen in the very deer park of the town of Peterborough and in all the woods that stretch from that same town to Stamford, and in the night the monks heard them sounding and winding their horns. Reliable witnesses who kept watch in the night declared that there might well have been as many as twenty or thirty of them winding their horns as near they could tell. This was seen and heard from the time of his arrival all through Lent and right up to Easter."

Most accounts agree in the description of the hounds, usually they are as large as a small calf. Their eyes are said to be flaming, fiery, blazing or glowing and are as large as saucers, normally red but sometimes yellow. They make little or no noise and usually all you can hear is the soft pad of their feet as they follow you. They appear from nowhere and can disappear just as quickly either by fading away, vanishing as you look away briefly or even sinking into the earth. Some have even been known to vanish with a flash or explosion (though this sounds more like a stage magician's trick). A lot of the descriptions are confused but this is probably due to the shock engendered in the person who sees them. The only thing that is certain in the descriptions is that when you see one you will know it.

In Norfolk there is an old saying that refers to these hounds. It goes as follows 'And a dreadful thing from the cliff did spring, And its wild bark thrill'd around, His eyes had the glow of the fires below, Twas the form of the Spectre Hound'.

The hounds are usually associated with a particular area, most often outside in rural areas but sometimes even indoors. They will haunt roads, crossroads, gallows and burial sites and are quite often seen near water. Bedfordshire's own Black Shuck (Galleytrot) haunts the roads around Millbrook to the west of Ampthill in the middle of the county. To encounter one of these hounds is generally thought to be a sign that someone (you or a member of your family) will die within twelve months; this is what happened to the unfortunate woman who saw one at Millbrook.

East Anglia is full of tales of spectral hounds with reports such as fishermen hearing a hound howling on the cliff tops near Sheringham on stormy nights, and one was even seen running along the beach at Great Yarmouth. In 1890 one young boy had to be rescued from the sea just off the coast of Norfolk. He said that he had to swim further and further out because of a huge black dog that had chased him into the sea. Some sightings can be dismissed as being of natural and not supernatural origin; just because you see a black dog at night doesn't mean to say it has to be Black Shuck. Any animal met during the dark of night appears black and larger than life, and glowing eyes can easily be due to a nearby street light shining in its face. Nonetheless many tales have a supernatural basis which cannot easily be dismissed. One such tale comes from Bungay in Suffolk and is dated 1577. Local parishioners were in the church when a violent storm erupted. The sky became black and the church is said to have quaked. Suddenly a large black dog appeared amidst the congregation and began running through the church. Two people who were kneeling in prayer were killed instantly as the dog ran between them. Another man was severely burned. At almost the same time another hound appeared in the church at Blythburgh striking three people dead and leaving scorch marks on the door to the church. This is a rare instance when the hound has brought instant harm and even death.

The name 'shuck' is thought to derive from Norse mythology and is based on 'Shukir', the huge dog of war that belonged to Odin and Thor. Other historians believe the name is derived from the Anglo-Saxon 'scucca' which meant a demon or devil. In Hrothgar's epic poem Beowulf the word appears in association with the monster Grendel, "scuccum ond scimmum" ('Shucks and Shines'), though its true meaning is not very clear. Whatever the origin the tales of the phantom hounds are some of England's oldest legends dating back over a thousand years.

Mythology says that the hounds haunt old roads that follow leylines, paths of invisible earth energy that run in straight lines across the country. Churches are often sited on these lines which, it is said, could be used by a spirit to travel from one graveyard to the next. Because of this they were sometimes called 'Corpse Ways'. Paranormal explanations would suggest that the hounds are the spirits of former working dogs or dogs that suffered cruelty and violent deaths. It may even be possible for the spirit of a person to materialise in animal form.

In general, however, encounters with these hounds are not an omen of death or bad luck. In Lincolnshire these dogs are believed to be harmless and even protective. Over the last one hundred years encounters with them have tended towards the friendly side of things, with many people greeting them as if they were some local pet out for a walk. This could be because a lot of the encounters are with real dogs and people today do not tend to overreact and convert a pet seen at night into a hound from hell. It is even suggested that the hounds are just stories to frighten children and grave-robbers. Parents may have told tales of spectral dogs to keep their children away from danger (a lot of the tales relate to water). Tales of spectral hounds near graveyards would have kept grave-robbers away. Some hounds have been seen by more than one person at the same time and the description precludes a normal dog.

BLACK SHUCK

A tale is told in the village of Uplyme, a few kilometres to the north of Lyme Regis in Devon. The tale shows that not all encounters with these dogs are bad; in fact this one was positively beneficial. The tale was first published in 1866 and tells of a farmer who lived in a cottage in the area. Every night a large black dog would appear in the cottage and settle itself down in the corner by the chimney. At first the farmer was shocked, but after a while he became accustomed to the presence of the dog, and almost welcomed its company. His friends and neighbours thought that he should chase it away, to which he replied "Why should I? He costs me nothing, he eats nothing, he drinks nothing, he interferes with no one. He is the quietest and frugalest creature in the house."

The association continued for a while, but one night the patience of the farmer snapped and seizing a poker he chased the dog out of the room. He pursued the dog around the house and in either the porch or an attic room the dog made a sudden leap upward through the ceiling. As the dog leapt, the farmer struck at him with the poker, but he only succeeded in making a hole in the plaster. Much to his surprise gold and silver coins began falling from the hole and forming a heap on the floor. The coins were old ones from the reign of Charles I. There were so many coins that the farmer was able to purchase the cottage opposite and open an inn, which he named after the dog. From then on the dog was still seen in the area, but only patrolling nearby Dog Lane (Haye Lane).

Whatever the explanation might prove to be, these hounds are seen from the USA to Croatia and Scandinavia to Italy. "In the beginning of January, 1905, about half-past seven in the evening, I was walking up from the Halfway [a local inn]. I suddenly saw an animal that seemed to be like a large, black dog appear quite suddenly out of the hedge and run across the road quite close in front of me; I thought it was the dog belonging to the curate. I was just going to call it to send it home, when it suddenly changed its shape, and turned into a black donkey standing on its hind legs. This creature had two glowing eyes, which appeared to me to be almost as big as saucers. I looked at it in astonishment for a minute or so, when it suddenly vanished. After that I hurried home, for the sight of this creature with the large shining eyes gave me a shock. The evening was a light one for the time of year."

Black Shuck has even found its way into popular fiction. In March 1901 Sir Arthur Conan Doyle returned from South Africa where he had contracted enteric fever. Doyle chose to recuperate at the Royal Links Hotel in Cromer, Norfolk, where he was told the tale of Black Shuck by his friend Bertram Fletcher Robinson. Doyle was so fascinated by the tale that he used it as the basis for the 'Hound of the Baskervilles' which he wrote in 1902. By the time he started writing the book Doyle had moved from Norfolk to Dartmoor, so he used that as the setting for the story. The house, Baskerville Hall, was relocated to the windswept and desolate Dartmoor but the description of it still matches Cromer Hall. Interestingly, the owner of Cromer Hall, Doyle's friend Bertram Fletcher Robinson, just happened to have a manservant named Henry Baskerville. Henry appears in the book as the heir to the estate and new owner of Baskerville Hall after the death of the previous owner (which was caused by the legendary hound of the title).

Even industrialised Luton had its tale of a hound from hell which was seen in the early part of the eighteenth century. At that time there was a gallows on Galley Hill to the north of the town, along with a gibbet from which the bodies of the criminals would be hung as a warning. A warning can only act as a warning if people are aware of it, so to make sure the bodies lasted they were first soaked in tar. One night a terrible storm hit the town with strong winds and tremendous bolts of lightning but surprisingly little rain. As Galley Hill is one of the highest points around it attracted the lightning which soon struck the bodies which were hanging on the gibbets in chains. The tar ignited and soon the whole hill was ablaze with flames leaping up into the sky. As the flames leapt higher the locals were terrified to see a large black dog which was virtually dancing around the flames. As the bodies burned it continued to prance around until all that remained were ashes, whereupon the dog gave out a long, bone numbing howl and vanished. The locals were convinced that the dog was a hound from hell. Since then the dog has returned on odd occasions, causing great dismay to those who have seen it. Apparently if you turn and flee you will live to tell the tale, but those who have chosen to approach the hound have never been seen again. Some hounds may be a good omen but the Hell Hound of Luton is not one of them.

The Reverend Worthington-Smith wrote a book entitled 'Dunstable: its history and surroundings' which was published in 1910. In it he wrote 'Another belief is that there are ghostly black dogs, the size of large retrievers, about the fields at night, that these dogs are generally near gates and stiles, and are of such a forbidding aspect that no one dare venture to pass them, and that it means death to shout at them. In some places the spectral dog is named 'Shuck' and is said to be headless'.

Across the country the hound has been given various names and below is a list of just some of them:

Devon	Yeth
Ireland	Pooka
Isle of Man	Moddey Dhoo
Jersey	Le Tchan de Bouôlé
Lancashire	Trash, Guytrash, Skriker
Leicestershire	Shag Dog
Lincolnshire	Hairy Jack
Midlands	Hooter
Norfolk	Old Shuck, Black Shuck, Norfolk Shuck, The Shug Monster
Scotland	Muckle Black Tyke, Choin Dubh, Cu Sith
Somerset	Gurt Dog
Staffordshire	Padfoot
Suffolk	Old Shock, Scarfe, Gally-trot, Gallytrot, Galley Trot, Moddey Dhoe
Wales	Gwyllgi
Warwickshire	Hooter
Westmorland	Cappel
Yorkshire	Barguest, Barghest, Barghaist, Barn-ghaist, Skriker

Chapter 3

How to Investigate

On these pages I will try to give you some ideas on how to go about an investigation and what equipment you might require. The extent to which you conduct an investigation is up to you; you can simply hold a vigil or you can go in for the full blown scientific study, the choice is yours. By a vigil I mean simply being at the haunted location and opening yourself up to whatever is there. You can choose just to walk a haunted road or maybe extend things slightly by placing a sound recorder near a haunted location and leaving it for a while whilst you investigate elsewhere.

If you go to the Equipment section you will find a fairly comprehensive list of equipment you could use, varying in price from a few £s to several hundred £s. Most of the equipment you already possess but in a less accurate form - yourself. On the list you will find thermometers (you are one, not very accurate but you can sense changes in temperature) and charge/EMF meters (you are these as you can sense static charges and changes in EMF as these tend to affect how you feel, which is why we buy ionisers for our homes). But most of all you can sensitise yourself so that you can feel the presence of a spirit, as you can see, hear and smell things that machinery will not pick up.

The Method section tells you briefly how I conduct investigations. These are never hard and fast rules, they are only guidelines; you should find the methods which suit you and are appropriate to what you seek. By this I mean what it is that you want to get out of an investigation. If you are only interested in seeing something and not recording the event then all you need is yourself. You should be aware that most ghosts are heard or felt, and not seen, so even a simple sound recorder can be enough equipment to start with.

Finally (or should this have been firstly) go to the Warnings section. The warning is there to make you aware of possibilities ('There are more things in Heaven and Earth, Horatio, than are dreamt of in your philosophy' – William Shakespeare).

EQUIPMENT

Below is a list of possible paranormal research equipment. The list is not a full one but should cover most of the equipment you are ever likely to need.

Air Pressure Meter

As the name suggests, an Air Pressure Meter detects changes in the local air pressure which may be associated with a manifestation. The simplest form of meter is a weather barometer which measures local pressure in an attempt to predict the weather.

Batteries

Every bit of equipment you use should be powered by batteries so that they can be used anywhere, at short notice and do not contribute much to the local electric and magnetic fields like mains powered equipment does. Because of this make sure you carry spare batteries. I always use high capacity NiMH batteries as they are rechargeable, so they save you money in the long run and can supply a lot of power (1800mAh or better for AA size).

In addition do not keep all of the spares on you but keep some nearby. This is because it has been recorded that a manifestation will drain the power from batteries and you don't want all of yours to go flat at the same time.

Camera

Vital for recording what happened. A camera can be an old style film camera, a digital camera or a camcorder (digital or tape storage). One of the most critical things is keeping the lens of the camera clean. When you clean the lens try to use a lens cloth as it picks up the grease. Tissues etc. may remove the grease but they leave fibres (instant orbs in the making).

Make sure you have enough memory in a digital stills camera to takes loads of pictures; you will be surprised how many you can get through (50 or more in an hour). Also make sure you carry spare batteries as they will not last long if you are using the flash all the time. Most cameras and camcorders come with screens so that you can see what it sees. This can be very useful as you may spot something on the screen which is not visible with the naked eye. This is especially true of the NightSpot cameras which can record in the absolute dark using infrared.

Dictation Machine

These are mini tape recorders or digital recorders that can be used to record what you are doing. A lot of people prefer the old notebook and pencil but the Dictation Machine has the advantage that you don't necessarily have to see to use it. Because of this you can record your observations and thoughts in the dark. Many types are voice activated, some with a variable level, so you can turn it on and leave it on but it won't record until you speak. If you don't want to hold it, most come with lapel microphones so you can keep it in your pocket set for voice activation and just talk when you need to. The digital ones have the advantage of being able to record lower sound levels without hearing the whirring from the tape.

Dowsing Rods

Dowsing rods are used to detect electromagnetic fields, using the rods as a conductor and yourself as the detector. They can prove to be useful in eliminating things such as underground streams as sources  of electromagnetic fields in an area you are investigating. In general the best rods are made of copper and are free to rotate as you hold them. Dowsing rods are not easy to use, so you should practise a lot before using them as part of an investigation.

Using them I would walk a site during the day, noting any responses and using a GPS receiver to note the location. When I return for the paranormal investigation I then know where there are areas which may affect my equipment.

EMF Meter

The Electro-Motive Force meter detects the presence of electric and magnetic fields in the environment. Many of these meters can be set so as to screen out the natural background EMF and even the higher levels that are found in a building and near electric and electronic equipment. Meters can have an audible alarm which triggers when a field which is stronger than a pre-set limit is detected. This allows you to leave it in a room and go off somewhere else to investigate. If a large enough EMF is detected the alarm will sound.

As there are many naturally occurring sources of EMF (including the human body) you need to get used to how these meters work so as to avoid false alarms.

These meters can be used to detect the presence of a spirit as it is believed they disrupt the local fields. Spirits need energy to manifest and this could include electricity. The meter can detect the changes in the EMF in the surroundings whether the spirit is absorbing or even generating the field.

Most EMF meters only work at 50 to 60Hz as they are designed to detect mains signals, but who says that ghosts only absorb/emit EMFs at 50 to 60MHz, which may limit their effectiveness.

Environment Meter

This instrument can be used to measure humidity levels, temperature, light and sound levels. It has the disadvantage that temperature has to be measured by making direct contact with the object.

Like other equipment this instrument should be used at the start of the investigation to measure humidity etc. all over the site. It can then be used to look for changes which may be associated with a manifestation.

GPS Receiver

The GPS or Global Positioning System receiver uses information from a large series of satellites in orbit above the earth to work out where it is and how high above sea level it is. Receivers can be very accurate and will certainly give you your location down to ten metres or less. Many also have the ability to be programmed so that you can use them to plan a route and even to back track a route you walked so you can find your way home. They can also be used to note the location of an event so that you can find the exact spot in the future.

They do not operate overly well in some buildings as they need a reasonably clear view of at least two satellites but will, in general, work in most locations. The more satellites the receiver can lock on to the more accurate the displayed location will be. With three satellites you can also obtain height data (so you will not only know where a site was but how far above the sea level datum it was).

Infrared Torch

An infrared torch uses either a series of infrared diodes or a bright light source like a Krypton bulb and a special filter. Infrared lies just beyond the red end of the visible spectrum and is used in most TV and video remote controls. No visible light can be seen from an infrared source except a red glow from a filtered Krypton bulb. Infrared light is detectable using night vision goggles or a charge coupled device which is the main constituent of digital and video cameras. If you use a strong enough source you will be able to see what is going on around you using the screen on your camera, even though the area appears pitch black to the naked eye.

You can buy torches with built in filters or you can buy sheets of filter material and create your own infrared source.

Ionisation Meter

This detects the levels of charged ions in the area including static electricity. Most ions are usually positively charged but it has been found that there are negative ions present when a paranormal event occurs. As with other meters this instrument should be used to take baseline readings of the area before the investigation starts so that you can see changes. The instrument will detect increased ionisation due to thunder storms, so it is a difficult instrument to use without practice. It will also detect the ionising effects of radiation and the presence of Radon gas.

Lightning Detector

This meter is capable of detecting lightning strikes out to a distance of fifty kilometres. It is useful as an approaching storm ionises your surroundings and will give you false results when you are using an ionisation meter.

If the Lightning Detector indicates that there are storms around then you will know not to believe the ionisation meter (you will also know that you may be about to get wet if you are working outside, and it will warn you that maybe now is not the time to be standing under a tree).

Maps/Plans

These will either allow you to reach your destination or will be used as part of the research for a site. Maps can be modern Ordnance Survey ones which will help you locate sites, or older maps which will show you how the landscape used to be. Older maps may show the location of buildings which have now been replaced by more modern ones. It could be that an apparition walks through a wall of the building, but by looking at the old map you may find the route used to be that of a road.

Plans for buildings, especially those of buildings which used to be on a site, can help you understand why an apparition does what it does. Ghosts have no respect for modern features and will walk through walls if they are in the way; old plans can again give you a clue as to the route they take.

Marble and Talcum Powder

No, this one is not for playing games. A combination of a marble and talcum powder can be used as a simple detector for psychic activity. First of all you dust talcum powder over a surface, then carefully place the marble in the centre. Don't use too much talcum powder as only a light dusting is sufficient. Also make sure that the marble is grease free. You can then leave the area and return later to see if the marble has been moved, as the trail will show up in the talcum powder. If you use too much powder it may end up stopping the marble from moving; in addition grease on the marble will pick up talcum powder and again stop the marble from moving. It is known that wood is a conductor for psychic energy, so you could place the marble on a small wooden table suitably dusted with talcum powder. The marbles I use are made from natural minerals like Hematite, Rose Quartz etc.

Motion Detector

These are usually Passive Infrared (PIR) and can be used to monitor a room for movement. Usually the detector would be set to cover as much of a room as possible or just to cover a small area. In the latter case the field over which the detector works can be reduced by covering part of the sensor window with aluminium foil. Avoid covering open doorways as a member of your team may walk past and inadvertently trigger the alarm (unless you feel you need to monitor that area, then remind your colleagues to keep away).

Night Scope

A Night Scope is basically an infrared light source and a viewer like a telescope. It allows you to see in absolute darkness without having to fill the room with visible light.

Images you see will be coloured in shades of green. This is because a single colour like green has little effect on your eyes' night sensitivity, and green is the colour with which the eye can see the smallest differences in shading and contrast.

HOW TO INVESTIGATE

Notebook and Pen

If you are visiting a site and interviewing witnesses, then you will need to take notes, so don't forget a notebook and pen or, if you prefer, a dictation machine. You may also want to keep notes about your feelings and experiences while you are visiting a site. Remember, of course, that a notebook is not much good in the dark.

Pendulum

A pendulum can be used in much the same way as dowsing rods. It can be used to find underground streams and other features that may affect the results of your paranormal investigation. It can also be used over a map to ask questions about a site or even locate a site providing simple yes/no type of answers.

Red Light Torch

If you have ever watched films like 'The Hunt for Red October', then you will have seen that on military submarines etc. they always switch to red light during emergency situations. The reason for this is that you can see well in red light and it does not affect your night vision. After a while under red light conditions your eyes will become dark adjusted, so that if the light goes off you can still see (as long as there is a faint light). The same cannot be said of going from a bright light into the dark, when it will takes quite a while for your eyes to adjust.

Sound Recorder and Microphone

There are alternatives, as long as it records sound. It can be your video camera or it can be a dictation machine. The best type is a digital one, as this eliminates the sound of the tape playing which you get with tape recorders.

If you are trying to record supernatural sounds with a sound recorder, then use an external microphone, especially if you are using a tape recorder. Internal microphones tend to be limited on frequency range and threshold levels and will pick up the sounds from a tape recorder's motor etc. The microphone can either detect sound from all directions or you could use a parabolic directional microphone to localise sounds.

Stud Detector

Stud detectors are usually designed to detect metal nails and pipe work in walls and also electrical cables. With the electrical cables the detector senses the electric field around the cable and beeps accordingly. This is useful when you feel there is an electric field in the site and you want to eliminate natural sources like buried cables.

Tape Measure

If you are doing an investigation in a building or even outside it is some times recommended that you record the dimensions of the area in which you are working. In a room this could involve its shape and the positions of doors and windows. If you see something you should write down where it was with respect to the room, as it may be possible to relate the location to a previous room layout. The ghost which walks through a wall may be coming through what was once a door, and accurate location information will allow you to prove this.

The device can be a simple tape measure or an electronic version as in an ultrasonic measure. The latter is simple and easy to use, though a lot more bulky than a tape measure. It also has the disadvantage of only being able to measure the distance to a surface. Thus to measure the location of a door you have to record the distance with respect to a wall; you cannot measure from a point on a wall to another point on the same wall. Basically, the ultrasound needs something to reflect off, creating an echo.

Thermometer

The best type of thermometer is an electronic one which is capable of reading a local temperature very rapidly. These are used to detect changes in local temperature, as it is known that the presence of a ghost causes cold spots.

Before you start the investigation you should walk all over the site measuring the temperature, so that you get a baseline value for the average site temperature. Most of these thermometers are not overly accurate (only within a few degrees) and local temperatures can naturally change by a few degrees in a short period of time.

Infrared thermometers have the advantage of measuring the temperature of the air and they are not affected by the movement of the air. If you use an old-style mercury thermometer it will record a different temperature if it is sitting in a draught. In addition infrared thermometers measure the temperature of an object without actually touching it, and the measurement is almost instant.

Torch

OK, so this one may seem obvious and that's probably because it is. If you are visiting a dark site it is preferable to see where you are going, hence the torch. That said, you should only use a standard white or yellow light torch when you really need to, as it affects your night vision. As you know going from a bright area to a dark area results in your being able to see nothing until your eyes dark adjust.

Two Way Radio

Two way radios are highly useful if you are investigating a site, especially a large building, and you have split up into groups. If one group sees something they can quickly radio to the others to come and see without missing anything themselves.

Radios have a limited range, usually a few kilometres with no obstructions, which should be more than adequate for most sites. Many can be used with an earpiece, so that the sound from the radio does not distract the people around you. Try to get rechargeable ones to save on batteries and remember to set them all to the same channel and test them before you start the investigation.

Vibration Detector

A Vibration Detector normally measures the levels of vibration in three planes, using separate sensors. You can either set the sensors to measure vibration in each of the three planes or set them at slightly different locations to measure different vibrations. They should be checked before the investigation starts as they will detect the vibrations caused by passing traffic.

Voltmeter

The voltmeter I refer to here is a simple affair used as part of a home made detector. The meter is connected to a battery so that it measures the battery voltage. This is then left at a location that you wish to monitor for psychic phenomena. People have found that batteries in cameras etc. can suddenly become completely discharged when they should still have been well charged. This is felt to be caused by a spirit trying to manifest and drawing energy from its

surroundings. The meter draws very little current from the battery so will not be responsible for the batteries going flat. The image shows two batteries, only one of which is connected to the meter. If both go flat it is paranormal, if only the test battery goes flat there is probably a fault with the meter. This meter is also useful for checking the charge levels of the batteries you use in your camera and other equipment.

Wooden Table

It is known that wood is a conductor of psychic energy so it can be used to see if the suspected spirit can move it, or it can be used as a conductor to or from you. In addition you could place a marble on the table suitably dusted with talcum powder (see the Marble section above).

METHOD

When I investigate, all I often take with me is a torch and a digital camera. If I see something, then believe me I am going to want a picture of it. The torch is not there to illuminate the surroundings all the time; it is there so I can see where I am going when I am walking a strange, dark path in the middle of nowhere. Even then the torch is only lit when I really need it (just before you walk off the edge of the quarry which is completely invisible in the dark is probably a good time). The reason for this is that a manifestation can be a very dim thing and in strong torch light you could see nothing. A spirit takes energy from you and your surroundings to manifest and may just appear as a glimmer in the air; 1,000,000 candle power of torch light would swamp anything. In addition you need to dark sensitise your eyes and this takes a while to do. This can be partially overcome by fitting a red filter to the front of the torch, as red light does not affect your night vision. The torch I carry is a small one yet adequate to enable you to see. It is powered by two AA batteries as is most of the equipment I use. I have purchased loads of rechargeable NiMH batteries (1800 to 2300mAh) and use these all the time. In a very short period they had paid for themselves, as I would have used hundreds of standard alkaline batteries by now.

I like technology. I am a designer in a high tech industry but I still prefer to use myself as the detector. I like to sit or walk slowly and attune myself to the surroundings. I like to open myself up to possibilities and use nothing to distract my feelings. Bright lights, excessive chatter and noise are all distractions which can prevent you sensing what is going on around you. Many religions, those of the North American Indians and Wiccans/Pagans, attune themselves to nature and their surroundings.

Technology does have its place as it allows you to effectively be in more than one place at a time and to detect things that you yourself may not be able to sense. Motion sensors can warn you when something is happening elsewhere, a thermometer can confirm that the cold chill you are feeling is real. Use technology but rely mainly on yourself. When you are out in the field record what your instruments say, but don't forget to record your feelings as well. If you suddenly feel different than you did five minutes ago write it down! Recently one member of a team of researchers, whilst investigating a haunted cave beneath the Olde Salutation Inn in Nottingham, felt a tightness in her chest that she had not felt before or since (as she is only seventeen years of age I am fairly sure we can rule out a heart attack, especially as I know her – she is my daughter).

When you investigate a site try not to go mob handed. If you look at all the reported sightings they tend to have occurred when only one or two people were present. This may partially be due to the fact that you can't really get in touch with your surroundings in the middle of a crowd. Even when there are a lot of you it is still possible to find things, as I have located cold spots and had problems with electrical equipment at a site when there were twenty people present. These effects were large and could not be missed, but more subtle signs will only be detected away from the crowd.

Remember that there are thousands of reported haunted sites in the UK alone but there are very few photographs of ghosts. Above all don't be afraid of the unknown, if you see something don't be scared and run off; you are one of the few to have a genuine paranormal experience, investigate it.

A WARNING

OK, so maybe this should have been at the start of the chapter, but I would prefer you to have read the rest first so that this warning is less likely to put you off what is an absolutely fascinating subject.

It is said that ghosts and spirits cannot harm you and this is true, there is very little evidence of anyone being injured by a ghost. Ghosts don't throw objects around, that is the job of a poltergeist which is associated with the living, normally a highly emotional teenager or child, and not the dead. Most of the harm you could come to lies in your own mind, mainly due to fear of the unknown (or due to falling into a dark ditch at a dark site). I believe that spirits cannot harm you, yet I appear to have been affected by my first ever visit to Clophill, which may be a coincidence or it may be due to the calling up of evil that has taken place there.

At the end of February 2004 I visited the ruined church of St. Mary at Clophill. It was a cold, windswept night and I was accompanied by several other people. At the time we did not sense anything except for a deep feeling of cold within the nave of the church, but that was most likely caused by the wind. Yet the next day, just eight hours later, I awoke with a bad headache which continued day after day. The doctor put it down to a long term migraine caused by a recent bad bout of sinusitis and started treating it as such. Many months later the headaches continued and treatments had failed to have any real effect. So what was the cause; is it a coincidence or is there something evil lurking around the vicinity of the church as many people believe? Spirits may not harm you, but many people believe malevolent forms exist that will try to do you harm. After nine months the headaches became more of an irritation than a distraction.

One thing I do know is that the (possible) result of my first visit has not put me off returning and I have been back there three more times since, once during the day and twice during the so called Witching Hour with both my seventeen year old daughter and my thirteen year old son. Now my head only really hurts when I sneeze or cough, and this is more than adequately compensated for by the enjoyment I have had doing the investigations!

I do not fear the unknown; in fact, it is the unknown that I seek. I still go out on my own at night, walking footpaths which are reported to be haunted. You should always be aware of possibilities, but you shouldn't let this wariness turn into fear.

A good definition of fear is: F.E.A.R – False Evidence Appearing Real. This means that your mind creates a danger which may not even be there. Do not be afraid of the unknown and remember the old adage that 'there is nothing to fear except fear itself'.

Chapter 4

Orbs

You have been out on your first visit to a haunted site and you have returned with photographs, videos, sound recordings and loads more results. But is the bright light you see on a photograph a ghost, is the misty figure real? In the next three chapters I hope to be able to help you answer these and similar questions.

In this chapter I will try to give you some ideas about orbs. On the photographs you have taken you may see circular features which are quite bright, possibly transparent and which vary in size from quite small to up to ten centimetres across, or so it seems. One thing you do know is that they weren't there when you took the photograph. These are what people refer to as orbs. By the time you have read these pages you should know whether or not the image given on the right is a true spirit orb.

Many people believe that orbs are the manifestation of the soul of a departed person, essentially their spirit. Within the spirit is everything they were, their personality, intelligence, memories and emotions. A sphere is the simplest structure, the one that takes the least energy to create and maintain. A circle has always been used to represent eternity, no beginning and no end. Some people interpret the orb as the physical representation of the energy that the soul contains. For people who do not believe in a soul the spirit orb is the essence of that person, the thing that made that person unique. Some also believe that the orb is a spirit in motion, moving energy trapped in a sphere. When the orb stops, the energy is released and appears as ectoplasm. It is also believed that moving orbs can contain multiple souls which are released as separate orbs when the carrier orb stops.

But not all orbs are spirits; you have to eliminate the natural causes to leave the unexplained, the supernatural. Many naturally occurring 'things' can appear as orbs, including dust and moisture. It is only by careful experimentation and analysis that you can eliminate these as the sources of orbs in your photographs. Try taking a number (this can amount to scores and scores) of photographs of known 'things' until you get an idea of how they usually appear in the images. This is effectively what I have done and the results are given on the pages which follow.

I will not attempt to prove that spirit orbs don't exist and I will not attempt to prove that they do, but what I will do is provide evidence for and against. Spirit orbs are one of those things that a lot of people believe in and will believe in no matter what. I believe in possibilities. I do not dismiss orbs and not all orb occurrences can be easily explained.

DUST

So what does a dust orb look like? Take as an example the image on the right; here you see a typical orb as would occur in a lot of photographs that people take. This type of orb is only visible in flash photography and has a bright outer ring (not always complete), and a random internal structure. 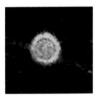 But this orb is man made. In

the image on the left you will see a large number of orbs. The orb in the first image is the one just to the left and below centre in the second image. The source of these orbs?...flour, a small pinch blown from an open hand a metre in front of the camera. This image was taken with a Kodak CX6200 camera, then enhanced using

Kodak Easyshare. The image of the flour was not taken immediately but a minute after the flour was blown. A picture taken just after the flour was blown revealed thousands of tiny specks, but after a minute the specks had turned into large orbs as the flour had dispersed and some had drifted towards the lens. Basically any dust orbs have to be close to the lens otherwise they appear as bright dots.

The very first image at the start of this chapter was taken indoors with a flash. If you take the orb and enhance it to increase the contrast

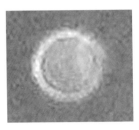

you get the image on the left. In the image you can see that the orb shows a very bright outer disk just inside of which is a darker disk. If you look carefully you will see that the dark ring is followed by a light ring then another dark ring and so on. All told the structure is similar to that of an onion. Another image which shows a

similar structure is given on the right; again it has the same light-dark-light bands. The difference between the two photographs is that the left hand ones' origin is unknown whilst the right hand one is talcum powder

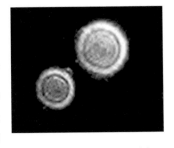

To try to explain these rings a series of photographs was taken of a small point in space from different distances. The point in space was the end of a sharp needle. Most of the photos revealed nothing except the outline of the needle, but some were orientated just right so that light reflected off the end of the needle. Whilst maintaining this

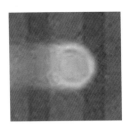

orientation the needle was moved closer to the camera lens from about five hundred millimetres away up to less than ten millimetres. When the needle was some way away all you got was a photograph of a needle, but as the needle got closer interesting things were seen. The image on the left shows a typical photograph from the needle experiment. When this photograph was taken the needle was only fifty millimetres from the lens and the rings are clearly visible. The light streak to the left of the rings is the shaft of the needle, so you can tell how close to the lens it must have been.

The camera used has a fixed focus lens which can focus from three hundred millimetres to infinity. It is only when the object is too close to the camera (a few centimetres or less), so that it is out of focus, that the

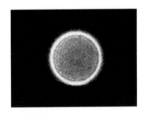

ring effect occurs. This effect can also be seen when using an astronomical telescope to view a star. When the star is out of focus it appears as in the image on the left, a bright outer disk complete with faint inner disks, just like the dust orb. The concentric rings are caused by diffraction which occurs as a result of the camera lens.

If a water wave hits a small hole the wave appears on the other side of the hole as a radiating wave front, a circular pattern centred on the hole. Light too acts as waves, so that a light beam hitting a small hole appears on the other side as a whole collection of waves. Water is made up of waves but light has the properties of both particles and waves. As light passes through the hole a radiating wave is produced from every point across the hole. Two of these radiating waves are shown in the diagram on the right. If two waves meet, the result will be the sum of both waves; if one

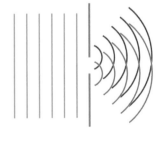

wave at a point is high and the other low the result will be nothing; if the

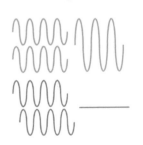

waves meet where the peak of one corresponds with the peak of the other the result will be a bigger peak. This can be seen in the diagram on the left

If you look at the light from the slit in terms of waves then the waves will add and subtract according to how they have been bent. The figure below shows this effect where a wave from the top of the slit meets a wave from the bottom of the slit, resulting in a wave which is the sum of the two. Whether the waves add to give a maximum or minimum depends on how far each has travelled from the slit. This addition and subtraction results in light and dark patches, looking like the plot to the right of the diagram on the left. If the slit is replaced with two objects very close together, then light reflecting off the objects can also interfere in the same way.

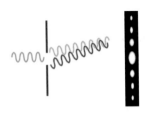

If the slit is a hole the pattern will form a circle known as an Airy Disk, as seen on the right. All you need for a diffraction pattern is a hole or aperture (think of the hole as a being made up of loads of little slits going round in a circle). This is exactly what you have on a camera, the lens. This hole is relatively large but still produces a faint diffraction pattern (the smaller the hole, the stronger the pattern). The Airy disk is the opposite of a dust orb disk, as it is based on light from an infinite distance away. Light which comes from a closer source or one that is out of focus produces the dust orb pattern of light on the outside and darker on the inside.

Some orbs may appear to be in motion, showing a distinct short trail. If the orb is dust and you are outside then this is likely, especially if the camera shutter is open for a long time. You may feel that the image must be an orb, as you distinctly remember that the wind was blowing from behind you yet the orb is travelling from right to left. As the wind blows around you it creates eddies, swirling air on the opposite side of the obstruction to that on which it is blowing. These eddies can create small amounts of air which can be travelling in any direction, even towards you. This being the case a dust orb close to the lens can also travel in any direction.

These images are not the only ones possible. You should test your own camera so that you do not fool yourself. One thing that should be noted is that all of these orbs require a light source (usually a flash, but even a street lamp or other strong light source might suffice). All are simple disks with little structure, controlled by the vagaries of the wind and usually uncoloured. Most orbs will also be white or slightly blue tinted, which is again due to the flash. If you have a picture of an orb and it is not almost white (with a hint of blue) then maybe, just maybe, you have something interesting.

MOISTURE

So what does a moisture orb look like? To see how artificial moisture orbs appear in my photographs I did a series of experiments by creating droplets of moisture and photographing them, in much the same way as I did the dust tests of the previous section. The droplets were created using a spray bottle, and the resultant mist photographed from various distances. With the mist one metre from the lens all that is really visible is a grey mist with a few brighter dots. If the test is repeated with the mist half a metre from the lens you can see 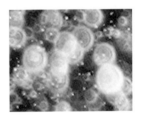 most of the droplets, appearing as bright dots on the image. But if you take a photograph very close to the mist you will see that the dots are no longer just dots. A close up of a group of moisture orbs from a photograph is shown in the image on the right. In general the ones which are slightly further away show a bright outer ring and a duller centre, some even show a series of light – dark – light rings. The orbs closer to the lens tend to be

 very bright and the structure is lost. If you compare these orbs with an artificially created dust orb you will find that they are very similar. In the image on the left the orb on the far left is moisture, the orb in the middle is dust and the orb on the right

is the same moisture orb but with the brightness reduced, so that the structure stands out. Generally from my tests moisture and dust orbs can appear almost the same but, in general, the moisture orb is brighter.

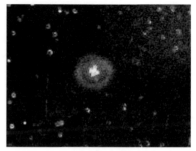

A very interesting, artificially created orb is shown in the image on the right. This one has a large outer disk surrounding what would appear to be several bright central dots. If you look at the original image you will see that, in this case, all of the moisture droplets appear as dots, implying that the mist is some way away from the camera. As orbs normally only occur when the object is so close to the lens that it is out of focus (see the Dust section), this orb must be created by some other means. The clue comes from the fact that there appear to be several bright spots in the centre. What is happening in this case is that there are several objects close together, each of which is reflecting light back into the lens. When these objects are very close together the light from one interferes with the light from the other to produce a diffraction pattern. See the section on dust orbs for a fuller explanation. Thus it is possible to get very unusual orbs from dust or moisture. Basically you have to try out your camera to see what it produces so as to eliminate these false orbs from your investigations.

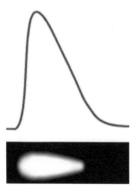

The way the flash operates on your camera also affects how a moving object appears. When the flash fires the light does not come on fully instantly, stay at the same level for a fixed time, then go off instantly. Instead the light level will rise quickly, reach a peak, and possibly remain there for a short time, then quickly fall. The curve at the top of the diagram on the left shows a possible profile for a flash. At the far left the flash is off, then the flash is fired and the light level rises very rapidly to a peak before falling back down slowly. This will result in a dust mote which is strongly illuminated at the start of its movement then less so as it moves across the field of vision. The brighter the particle is illuminated the larger it looks, so you end up with a streak which appears larger at the start and smaller at the end of its travel.

An example of an actual photograph containing streaks is given on the right. If you look at the image you will notice that the orb in the middle is streaked; this is a rain drop. The length of the streak depends on the size of the drop, how close it is to the lens and any prevailing winds. Basically the closer the drop the further it will appear to move on the image. In the image above the drop is wider at the top and narrower at the bottom. In reality the drop remains the same size and the apparent change is due to the camera. As explained above, as the flash fires the light reaches maximum intensity very quickly then slowly dies away. The result is a brief, bright light, then a slow dimming which makes the object appear bigger at the start of the flash.

If the streak moves to the side, then it was obviously windy as the droplet wasn't falling straight down. You may still feel that the image you have taken must be an orb, as you distinctly remember that the wind was blowing from behind you, yet the orb is travelling from right to left. As previously explained, the wind blowing around you creates eddies, swirling air on the opposite side of the obstruction to that on which it is blowing and which can be travelling in any direction, even towards you. Thus a moisture orb close to the lens can travel in any direction.

Remember that moisture can appear in many forms, all of which will give slightly different results on your photographs. Raindrops tend to be large and give big streaks; fog can be made of very small water droplets and will appear as orbs. Generally it isn't windy when it is foggy, so you are less likely to photograph a streak but you can get very good orbs.

Conclusion?

Now what do you think the orb in the picture at the start of this chapter is? If you answered 'dust' then you are right.

Well, I have shown you dust orbs and I have shown you moisture orbs, both of which bear a remarkable resemblance to the orbs which most people claim are spirit orbs. All show the same basic ring structure be it just one bright outer ring or a series of concentric rings. So is that it? Are all orbs dust or moisture? Most are, in fact they nearly all are, but one photograph in a few thousand may not be quite so easily dismissed. Orbs are not generally visible to the naked eye and require flash photography, but who is to say that a true spirit cannot take on the form of a solid but minute orb. Enough energy can be stored in the atomic structure of even a microscopic particle, so that it could contain a lifetime of knowledge etc. Take, for instance, a piece of wood from an oak tree, but only take a miniscule amount, say a piece one thousandth of a millimetre across. Now convert that tiny amount of mass into pure energy and you have enough to run a 60W light bulb for nearly a day, or enough to run you for one and a half weeks.

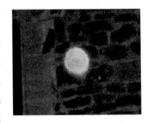

One last thing, look at the orb in the image on the right. This one shows a faint ring structure but it was very bright, appeared as big as someone's head in a full body photograph and is extremely yellow. The colour was very unusual as there was nothing in the area of similar colour and there were no other light sources around. The picture was taken outside St. Michael and All Angels at Millbrook which is a very dark site; there are no street lights in the area and there was no moon that night. So where did the colour come from? Maybe I need to extend my experiments to try to generate coloured orbs, possibly by using different materials like pollen grains?

The image above satisfies most of the artificial orb criteria yet it is still unusual looking. Now this is what I class as interesting because I am unable to explain it (yet)!

Chapter 5

Manifestations

According to Websters dictionary, a manifestation is 'The materialised form of a spirit'. A manifestation is what people classically think of as being a ghost, though usually they are thinking of a whole body, physical representation of a human form. Yet this is not the only thing a manifestation can be, and it is the other forms that I will talk about herein. I am not dismissing the whole body type, it is just that if you see a person who walks through a wall and you are not asleep, then it was probably really a ghost. I am talking about mists, vapours and other such more subtle manifestations.

I always want to know whether or not the thing I photographed is a paranormal phenomenon or not, so I first try to see if I can reproduce the effect, as I did with orbs in the preceding chapter. If you photograph a strange mist which looks paranormal but was in reality natural, then it was most likely to have been water vapour. This could either be your breath or a mist, but it could also be smoke (especially cigarette smoke). The latter creates traps which are easy to fall into, as smoke can travel hundreds of metres without dispersing. Because of this you should always avoid smoking if you are undertaking an investigation; anyway people have smelt tobacco smoke when there was no one else there, so you could possibly be masking a real phenomenon.

Smoke and breath may not be visible on a dark night when you are not using your torch all the time (which you shouldn't be) but, believe me, if there is any around, the flash on your camera will find it.

MOISTURE

Moisture from breath can take on some really weird and wonderful patterns in the flash from a camera, so always try to hold your breath as you take a photograph. In addition make sure no one is standing nearby, as their breath could blow across in front of your lens. 'Nearby' means within a few dozen metres, as breathe can travel a long way on the breeze. In fact it is safest to make sure that there is no one upwind of you before you take a picture. At night and even during the day given the right conditions, mist can rise from the ground, especially as the temperature and pressure drops. These mists can be very isolated, usually in spots where there is no wind, and can easily be misinterpreted by an active imagination.

The image that can be seen on the right is a prime example of a moisture manifestation. People have looked at this image and have said that they could see a knight on horseback (he is the wispy figure on the left and the horses' head is on the right). If you enlarge it then it is even more convincing; pity it was my breath.

In the image below is that a strange creature reaching out for something? No, it's my breath again! These are but two photographs which show something that isn't really there. Have you ever stared at the patterns on curtains (floral ones are the best) and seen a face appear in the pattern? Well that is what a lot of people do when they see a mist. They will look at the patches of mist and the dark shapes which show

through from the background and they will see whatever they like (skulls are very popular). I am not saying that every mist image is false, but a lot of times the thing you see will not show up to anyone else unless they really stretch their imagination, so be warned. In fact misty manifestations are rare, as most people see real representations of people, or if they do see a mist it is where it shouldn't and really couldn't be. A vapour which drifts down a hallway in a heated building where no one is smoking is what you are really after.

SMOKE

Smoke is the other bane of the paranormal investigator's life. I have stood outside Houghton House in Ampthill and smelt cigarette smoke, yet the nearest houses were down in the valley nearly three quarters of a kilometre away. Could it have been paranormal? I think not, as the smell was coming on the wind and would come and go as the wind eddied around. With the correct conditions the smoke itself can travel a long way and still remain visible. In the image on the right what is the strange light on the right of the  photograph? Is it energy? Is something trying to appear? Yet again the answer is no. This time it is smoke from burning incense.

I have seen numerous photographs of streaks of light which people claim are leylines (paths of energy which connect ancient sites), yet a lot look like photographs I have taken of smoke, hairs and spiders' webs.

In the image at the top of the next page can you see the torso of a woman? Sorry, it is again smoke (and if you can't see it when I can maybe I should consider therapy). The clue which really gave away the

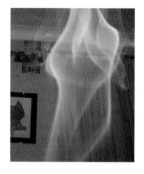

artificial nature of the second photograph is that you can see the same bat drawing on the wall (drawn by my daughter) as appears in the first image.

One thing that is very noticeable in the smoke images that I have taken is that the smoke needs to be very close to the camera lens, otherwise it looks like smoke. When it is seen very close it takes on lots of weird and wonderful shapes, but in all cases it is out of focus (though this helps add to the illusion). I have found that you need to be within about five centimetres to get the effects seen in the preceding images. If you see too large an area of smoke, it is obvious it is smoke.

FIBRES

One final corruptor of good paranormal photographs is fibres (hairs, wool and especially cobwebs). The image on the right is a window in Houghton House, Ampthill which appears to have a strange anomaly over it. There seems to be a white streak above the window which does not look natural. When this photograph was taken the air was very damp; it was not actually raining at the time, though it was certainly very misty.

Several other photographs taken at the time showed a grey mist and even on this one there are a few moisture orbs visible. But moisture would not explain the bright streak. So could this be paranormal? Is this a spirit in motion or could it be a leyline?

The image on the left looks very much like the Houghton House one. It starts as a faint patch at the top then brightens before fading towards the bottom. In the Houghton House image the pattern of faint-bright-faint is the same except it goes from right to left. The image at the top of the last page is, in fact, an artificial one. This one is a hair positioned about three centimetres from the camera lens. The hair is slightly curved so that only one bit faces directly towards the camera (the brightest bit) whilst the other bits are reflecting the light away from the camera, hence they are darker. This hair was a very thick black one so it can still be seen at the bottom left of the

image, but finer and lighter hair tends to vanish so you only see the illuminated bits. Spider's web is the best, as this really does give a bright streak fading to nothing at the edges

The last image on the left shows the same hair slightly further away; now it appears to consist of a string of what look like orbs. Basically you can get virtually any pattern you like, so be very suspicious of linear anomalies (long, thin and bright), especially when the spiders are breeding (baby spiders leaving the nest spin a long strand of silk which the wind catches and there by pulls them through the air).

OTHER CAUSES

One thing you should always do is keep your camera lens clean, as I discovered to my cost a long while ago. In the image on the right you will see a light patch just above and to the left of the large grave in the foreground. On the original photograph the patch is actually tinted red and looks very impressive. It took me some time to discover what it was, and when I did I wasn't very

happy with myself. The clue came when I looked at the other photographs I had taken just before and after this one, and the same red patch was on all of them, not only that but it was in the same position on each photograph. So what was it? I hate to admit it, but it was grease on the lens! I used to clean the lens several times a night, now I do it before virtually every photograph.

Insects can also be misinterpreted as something paranormal when they are seen later in a photograph that you took at a site during the night. If the insect is small and close to the lens it can take on any shape you want in the flash, especially if it is so close that it is out of focus. This is most likely to occur on dry nights in the spring and summer and least likely to occur in the depths of winter. I always remember taking a picture along the footpath at the end of Buttercup Lane in Dunstable. On the photograph there is a strange streak of light. It is only when you enlarge the photograph that you realise what it is. As you zoom in, the streak becomes larger and larger, then eventually it starts to grow legs and wings. It only looked like a streak, because the body was reflecting more light than the wings and legs.

Conclusion?

It is very easy to take a photograph which contains a bright streak like anomaly which can easily be interpreted as paranormal. Unfortunately, most of the streaks will have a natural origin, hairs, spider's web etc. It is worthwhile doing tests with your own camera so that you get used to the effects moisture and different fibres have, then you can eliminate these false images. Once you have worked out what can cause false images you will be better able to say whether the strange streak you have seen is other worldly.

Most objects when they are photographed at extreme close up (unintentionally of course) will show up as something weird, and then it only takes your imagination to turn them into something spooky.

When you take a photograph always be down to earth when you interpret what you see. Most of the strange things seen in photographs have a natural explanation; otherwise there would be literally millions of images which prove the existence of the paranormal!

Chapter 6

Noises

Noises associated with paranormal phenomena are a lot more common than visual effects. At a large number of haunted sites nothing is ever seen only heard, and of the audible phenomena footsteps are in the majority (to be strict the most common effect of a haunting is not through sight or sound but through feelings, the cold chills and the impression you get that you are being watched).

The problem with noises is that it is very difficult to eliminate natural phenomena as the cause, mainly due to the fact that most noises are short lived and difficult to localise. When you hear a sudden creak which direction did it really come from? Most of the time all you can say is 'that it came from somewhere over there'. Even then the sound could have come from above or below and the real direction is lost in the echoes and acoustics of the room.

A classic example of a ghostly sound with a natural cause was that affecting St. Michael and All Angels at Millbrook. Briefly, in 1857 restoration work was being done on the church and two statues of William and Mary Huett had to be removed. Unfortunately, the church ran out of money and the statues could not be restored. It is said that from then on the church echoed to the sound of creaks and groans which had no explanation. The villagers believed that the noises were caused by the Huetts who were angry that their statues had been removed. Then in 1888 the chancel roof collapsed and an investigation revealed that it was riddled with death watch beetle. This was the cause of the noises (though not all of the villagers were convinced). This was a case of don't believe everything you hear.

If you are investigating a sound, then you must make every effort to prove it has a natural origin. Sounds are elusive and the causes can be more so. Creaks and groans caused by a building slowly settling into the ground can sound very human at times. A cat wailing in the night can sound just like a baby crying. Even rhythmic noises, such as a click which repeats every few seconds, can have a natural source, in this case usually due to the cooling of a building after the heating has been on or the sun has warmed the roof space.

You should be cautious with recordings as the sounds are quite often distorted, especially if you use the internal microphone on a dictation machine. If you can, use a proper microphone and position it away from the machine, especially if it uses a tape to record sounds onto. I suggest this as a lot of the noise you will hear on a tape recorder is the sound of the tape moving and the motors whirring. If you are trying to pick up a faint sound it is no good if everything is drowned out by the sounds coming from the recorder itself. You can even use a directional microphone (a parabolic antenna looking like a small satellite dish with a microphone in the centre). This allows you to locate the direction a sound is coming from, remembering, of course, that the sound you hear might be an echo and not the original sound. This can be especially useful if you are recording the sound of footsteps.

Footsteps are the most common of the sounds, but natural sources of sound can be misinterpreted as footsteps. Footsteps are usually heard coming from the rooms overhead, but the sound could be coming from elsewhere in the building and is being conducted through the walls and floor. How often have you heard the sounds of people talking several rooms away? The sound does not (cannot) come direct to your ears; it has to be conducted. Such sounds tend to be muffled as only the low frequency end of the sound is conducted (high pitched sounds tend to be eliminated whilst low frequency sounds, like a lorry going by outside, make the walls and floors resonate, so they act like a speaker). A rhythmic creaking of a floor can sound like footsteps when heard from a distance, but the 'footsteps' will just be in one place (as the sound is not moving). If the sounds fade away, your mind, which thinks you can hear footsteps, will wrongly interpret the fading as footsteps which are receding. With a directional microphone you will be able to track the sound and confirm whether it is really moving.

Some sounds cannot be easily explained away, and really it is these you are looking for. Two sounds that I will always remember were recorded by me at a public house in Ampthill during an all night vigil. In the first sound you can hear one of the Luton Paranormal Society members talking to a male staff member of the pub with the strange sound over the top, almost like a demonic

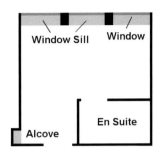

laugh. When the recording was made, the recorder (a tape dictation machine using its internal microphone which is all I had at the time) was placed on a ledge in a small alcove in the room (see the image above). The LPS member was sitting on the window sill on the left of the room and the pub staff member was sitting on the centre window sill. Another pub staff member was sitting on a chair between the left and central windows and two other LPS members were by the right hand window. The tape recorder had been set up by me, and I remember the conversation that was recorded (at the time I was standing about two metres from the recorder, the room being about five metres square). At no time do I remember anyone making any noises (coughing etc.) during that part of the recording. Yet the sound is there on the tape and it does not really sound like any noise anyone would have made, even allowing for the distortion of using the internal microphone and the echoing effects in the room (which was devoid of carpet and furnishings except for the plastic/metal chair).

The second recording was done in an unoccupied room, with the tape left on for approximately one and a half hours. This room was not one which any members of LPS entered until after the recording was complete. The room was very similar to the one given in the diagram above except that it is effectively a mirror image with the en suite on the left and the main door on the right. The windows at the far end of the room (opposite the door) face outwards onto Dunstable Street, which by then was deserted. The room is one floor up and to the right of the main entrance to the inn (which lies on the far left of the building). The recording was started at 0230 and from then on the only sound of the door opening was when I left the room. The doors are all heavy and very noisy, so, if the door had been opened, no matter how gently, the recording would have picked it up. At one point on the tape you can hear the muffled sounds of the LPS and staff members changing rooms; voices can be heard but they are very indistinct as the sounds are coming through the walls and floor. Then, as it goes quiet, you can clearly hear the distinct sound of a voice shouting "Get out!" twice, but the voice is very quiet as if it has come from some way away. The voice does not sound distorted, so it has not come through the walls or floor or even the window, it just sounds as if it has come from a long way away. Were we disturbing something that wanted us out of the building? In 2001 there had been a fire at the pub and the refurbishment was nearly complete when LPS visited; had the work disturbed something?

It is possible that the sounds were made by people playing tricks. But no one in the room at the time recalls any sounds even remotely similar to those on the first recording. On the second recording no one enters the room, so what was the source of the voice, as it does sound as if it is coming from within the room? In fact no one knew the second recording was being done apart from the three LPS members who were in the same team as I was. All four members of that team stayed together for the whole duration of the recording, so whose voice is it?

Some sounds that you hear may not even show up on a recording, because you are not hearing them with your ears. When a spiritual medium contacts a spirit he/she hears the voices (this depends on the mediums ability as many only get impressions and don't 'hear' anything), but someone standing alongside wouldn't. If you hear the sound on a psychic level it will most likely only be you who hears it. The term for this is 'clairaudience', which is defined by Websters dictionary as 'the power or faculty of hearing something not present to the ear but regarded as having objective reality'. It is known that a ghost can appear to just one or two people in a group but not the rest, implying visualisation on the psychic level (clairvoyance). The same applies to sounds (clairaudience), smells (clairessence - intuitively smelling that which is not present) and feelings (clairsentience - sensing something's presence or emotions). Communication and the ability to sense things at the psychic level could explain a lot of the sightings and why they are only seen by some people and not by others.

Remember that a lot of the sounds you hear will be natural; eliminate those and what is left just might be paranormal. If you are in the room where a recording is being made note down the time the recording starts, the time it stops and any sounds that you hear, along with the time. Then, when you listen to the tape later, you can relate any unusual sounds to those you heard yourself. If someone coughs, note the time, then, when you hear the strange noise on the tape at exactly the same time as the person coughed, at least you will know that it had an earthly origin.

Sound recording (especially Electronic Voice Phenomena – EVP) is the easiest of all the investigative methods and can provide some excellent results. Its greatest advantage comes from the fact that you do not have to be there while a recording is taking place. The advantage is two fold, firstly you can be investigating elsewhere at the same time, and secondly, the area being empty avoids some of the necessities of proving that the sound didn't come from you or anyone else present.

Conclusion?

Sound recording of paranormal phenomena is a lot less susceptible to misinterpretation than a photograph. Sometimes you will decide that you can hear a sound, like a voice, on a recording which is not really there (it is your imagination), but this is a lot less likely than misinterpreting a photograph.

The down side of sound recording is that it is very easy for someone other than you to create a false sound which then appears as the voice of a ghost on the recording. Because of this you should always try to ensure that other people cannot access an area where you are doing a recording; if they can then your recording will be invalid.

Appendix - Reading a Map

Throughout this book I have tried to provide the grid coordinates of each site to enable you to find it with the least hassle. As an example Houghton House just outside Ampthill is given as TL03923946. This is the British National Grid reference which allows you to locate any place in the United Kingdom with an accuracy that depends on how many digits there are in the number. Locating a point on a map from its reference or providing a reference from a map is easy and I will quickly tell you how.

The whole of the country has effectively been divided up into 100km squares and if you buy an Ordnance Survey Landranger map you will find it covers an area 40km square. Each of the 100km squares is given a unique two letter code and these appear on a Landranger map usually around the edges and look like the image on the right. This number is the first part of the grid coordinates, so that Houghton House lies in the TL square (so now you know where it is within 100km, but that is too inaccurate to be practical).

To provide a more accurate location the two letters are followed by numbers starting with a minimum of four and going upwards, the more there are the more accurate a position will be. Each group of numbers should be divided into two (two groups of two numbers for a four digit number, two groups of three for a six digit number etc.). The first set of numbers tells you where you are across the map going from left to right (eastings as you are going east) the second set tells you a location going up the map (northings as you are going north). The diagram on the left shows how the grid is labelled. On the map the 100km grid is divided up into 1km squares, with each square being marked out in pale blue and appropriately labelled (always in pairs from 00 on the left or bottom up to 99 to the right or top).

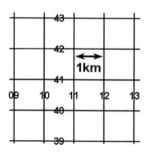

To give a grid reference to the nearest 1km simply write down the two letter code for the 100km grid (TQ) followed by the number on the grid line to the left of the square in which the site is located followed by the number on the grid line to the bottom of the square in which the site is located. On the diagram above the 1km label is in the square which has 11 on the left and 41 on the bottom so the grid reference would be TQ1141.

To give a more accurate reading you take the 1km square and divide it down again, so that it consists of 100 little squares each 100m across, as can be seen in the diagram on the right. Here the grid square TQ1141 from before has been divided up into ten horizontal and ten vertical sections. This new 10 by 10 grid has a zero for eastings to the left so that the original pale blue map line labelled '11' becomes the starting point (0). To give eastings for the black filled square just work out the number of the line on the left of the square, in this case 3. The same applies to northings counting up from the nearest pale blue line below the black square (41) to get an answer of 4.

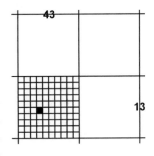

The easiest way to work out the grid reference to the nearest 100m is to write down the two letters (TQ) from the edge of the map (the nearest letter to the left and below the site), then to use a ruler. First of all find the nearest pale blue grid line to the left of the site (11) and measure how far the site is in millimetres from that line using a ruler. Say you get 7. Divide that by two, 3.5, then ignore everything to the right of the decimal point, 3. You divide by two because each pale blue square is 1km wide and measures 20mm on the map. Thus 2mm on the map equals 100m on the ground. So now you have TQ113. Do the same thing again starting with the pale blue line below the site (41) and measuring how far the site is above that line, say 9, divide by 2, 4.5 and round it down to 4. Thus you now have 414 to be added to the TQ113 to give TQ113414. If you want to give the location more accurately, then you can further divide the small squares into a hundred smaller squares to give a position accurate to 10m.

Further Reading/Websites

This book is intended as a brief list of a large number of the haunted sites around Bedfordshire, without going into excessive detail. If you require a more in-depth account of some of the sites, or you want to know more about ghosts in general, then I recommend you read some of the following books, or visit some of the websites whose addresses are given below.

Books

Ghosts of Bedfordshire
Betty Puttick - Countryside Books - 1996

Haunted Places of Bedfordshire and Buckinghamshire
Rupert Matthews - Countryside Books - 2004

Ghostly Bedfordshire
Damien O'Dell - Egon Publishers Ltd - 2004

Seeing Ghosts
Hilary Evans - John Murray (Publishers Ltd.) – 2002

An excellent book which details hundreds of paranormal events from around the world. Hilary analyses the causes, then tries to explain the paranormal.

The Good Ghost Guide
John Brook - Jarrold Publishing – 1994

A good general list of haunted sites throughout Great Britain.

Things That Go Bump in the Night
Emily Peach - Aquarian Press – 1991

This book helps you to better understand the ghost experience by explaining the effect these phenomena have on people, animals and machinery.

Websites

In addition to the sites listed below, it is worth exploring the websites of many of the towns and villages mentioned in this book, as quite a few contain local stories about ghosts and other phenomena.

www.mysteriousbritain.co.uk
A database of many of the paranormal phenomena across the country.

www.paranormaldatabase.com
Another database of many of the paranormal phenomena.

www.spr.ac.uk
The Society for Psychical Research. The oldest group examining paranormal phenomena.

www.lutonparanormal.com
The Bedfordshire group of which I am a member.

www.ghostclub.org.uk
The Ghost Club. One of the longest established paranormal investigation societies in Britain.

www.parasearch.org.uk
Not a local group, but the site contains interesting information about how to undertake a vigil, orbs etc.

Acknowledgements

I would like to thank all of the people who have contributed to this book both by way of stories and through their support. I would like to particularly thank my son and daughter who aided me in my investigations and who sense a lot more than I do. A final thank you must go to the members of the Luton Paranormal Society who have made many of the investigations fun and who have helped expand my knowledge of the paranormal and other aspects.

Index

EXPLORING HISTORY ALL AROUND

Vivienne Evans

This handbook of local history, arranged as a series of routes to cover Bedfordshire and adjoining parts of Hertfordshire and Buckinghamshire is organised as two books in one. There are seven thematic sections full of fascinating historical detail and anecdotes for armchair reading. Also it is a perfect source of family days out as the book is organised as circular motoring/cycling explorations, highlighting attractions and landmarks. Included is a background history to all the major towns in the area, plus dozens of villages, which will enhance your appreciation and understanding of the history that is all around you!

The
Book
Castle

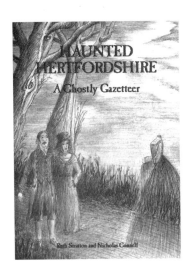

HAUNTED HERTFORDSHIRE

Nicholas Connell and Ruth Stratton

The most extensive collection of the county's ghosts ever written, with over 300 stories. Many are little-known and previously unpublished, having been hidden away in the vaults of Hertfordshire Archives and Local Studies. Others are up to the moment accounts of modern hauntings in the words of those who have experienced them. All supported by dozens of rare and evocative pictures, an outline of the latest theories and diary dates of regular apparition appearances.

Stories feature a feast of phantoms, including grey ladies, dashing cavaliers, spectral transport, headless horsemen and a gallery of Kings and Queens.

Locations include Bishops Stortford, Datchworth, Harpenden, Hertford, Hitchin, Hoddeson, St. Albans, Ware and Watford.